Direct
action and liberal
democracy

By the same author

The Political Theory of Anarchism

Direct action and liberal democracy

April Carter

Harper & Row, Publishers
New York, Evanston, San Francisco

Direct action and liberal democracy

Copyright © 1973 by April Carter

Library of Congress Catalog Card Number: 73-5675

Standard Book Number: 06-136129-1

Contents

Acknowledgments

My general intellectual debts to past colleagues will be recognized by any of them who read this book, but are too numerous and too diffuse to be acknowledged here. Specifically I am very grateful to Margaret Canovan, Paul Brodetsky and Fay Gadsden for advice on various parts of this book, to Eileen Brock for her help with typing, and to David Hoggett for lending me so many books from the Commonweal postal library.

Introduction

The last two decades show a startling contrast in political styles. In the calm of the apparent political apathy of the 1950s political commentators took for granted the age of liberal consensus and parliamentary compromise. A political and theoretical challenge to the supremacy of this brand of liberalism emerged early in the 1960s. This challenge grew out of the movements against the H-bomb, against racialism and later against the Vietnam war. The broader challenge was developed by the grouping usually called the 'New Left', which by the mid-1960s began to reject more explicitly the values of 'liberalism'. The alienation of the New Left from western society was both increased and extended by the development of a youth 'counter culture' in the same period.

Any theoretical discussion of the challenge posed to liberal democracy must involve an analysis of the methods adopted by protest movements which have, to a large extent, discarded orthodox liberal styles of political activity for various modes of 'direct action' such as 'sit-downs', 'sit-ins', civil disobedience and draft-resistance. The political implications of direct action depend, however, not only on what types of action are taken, but on the aims of the movement and the response of the authorities. Above all, perhaps, the political implications of direct action depend on the precise social context in which it takes place—whether, for example, in the Deep South or in the Ivy League universities.

This book concentrates primarily on examining the nature of the 'direct action' which typified the style of protest movements in the 1960s. Examination of the method is therefore necessarily entwined with the evolution of these movements. But direct action is also treated as a mode of political activity which has a much longer history, and draws on a number of different traditions. It therefore transcends the specific associations of movements like the New Left. And on the evidence available so far, direct action looks as though it may become in the 1970s a method increasingly used by large numbers of people impatient of waiting for the authorities to act on their behalf. If so, it will, as in the past, be an instrument of popular radicalism; and the spread of direct action tactics may be one aspect of the populist mood which seems to be replacing the mainly student dissent of the 1960s.

The later chapters consider some of the liberal arguments against direct action, and the various liberal or democratic justifications for extra-constitutional forms of protest. This discussion does not attempt anything so ambitious as a total critique of western parliamentary democracy —or a full discussion of the complex theory of liberalism. Instead, it explores a few limited themes in relation to the role of direct action in a parliamentary system, and the implications of such action for both parliamentary democracy and a liberal society.

1 The meaning of direct action

Direct action is currently a popular but somewhat ambiguous term. It suggests that people are taking to the streets, having abandoned the processes of discreet lobbying in the corridors of power. But a conventional march through the streets of London—which has become a standard pressure group tactic—would not today count as 'direct action', since direct action is associated with sit-downs and arrests, or with violent confrontations with the police.

Direct action cannot, however, be defined solely in terms of the methods used. It depends also on the political context and on the mood surrounding the event. Holding a march in defiance of a banning order, or as a form of demonstration in a situation of mass unrest, might well constitute direct action.

The purposes of direct action are also extremely varied. It may involve an attempt to assert what are regarded as basic constitutional rights—for instance, holding a meeting. It may be a more dramatic substitute for lobbying the government, but have the same goal: to bring pressure to bear in order to attain a limited and specific reform. It may be designed to demonstrate in action the answer to a particular problem—homeless families squatting in empty council houses, for example. It may be primarily a symbolic act of protest or solidarity in relation to a wider struggle, for instance, a boycott of South African goods. Or it may be a method used to repudiate the entire political system and promote insurrection.

Strict definition of direct action in terms of method, goal, or of the persons using it is likely to become sterile and misleading. But if it is not to shade off into meaninglessness, it must be distinguished from constitutional and parliamentary styles of activity on the one hand, and from guerrilla warfare on the other. Neither is direct action simply a synonym for protest or for violence, though it is closely associated with protest movements, and may result, unintentionally or intentionally, in some forms of violence.

The most illuminating approach to an understanding of what is entailed in the idea of direct action is to consider which movements have consciously used direct action, and what theoretical connotations surround their use of the phrase. This chapter therefore draws on the writings of advocates of direct action, and on studies of particular direct-action campaigns.

The major influences on the current conception of direct action have been anarcho-syndicalism; the western adaptation of Gandhian non-violence in the civil rights protests in the United States and in demonstrations against nuclear weapons; the evolution of the movement against the Vietnam war; the student movements of the late 1960s; and political manifestations of youth counter-culture, for instance, the 'Provos' in Holland and the 'Yippies' in the United States. In the past few years there has also been a growing tendency for groups without any conscious theoretical commitment to direct action to resort to forms of physical intervention or civil disobedience in order to make the streets safe for their children, to preserve or improve the amenities of their community, or to gain a home for their families. This tendency has spread to workers in Britain faced with the threat of unemployment, who have resorted to new forms of militant industrial action to safeguard their jobs.

Anarcho-syndicalism

The anarchist and syndicalist traditions are perhaps the earliest, but most continuously significant, contribution to the present theory of direct action. Daniel Guérin in his recent book on *Anarchism* quotes the Russian anarchist Voline:

> True emancipation can only be brought about by the direct action ... of those concerned, the workers themselves, through their own class organizations (production syndicates, factory committees, cooperatives, etc.) and not under the banner of any political party or ideological body (37).

In their account of the events of May 1968 Daniel and Gabriel Cohn-Bendit, who consciously relate themselves to Kronstadt and to Makhno's anarchist movement in the Ukraine in 1918–21, illustrate this theme:

> Perhaps the most concrete expression of this new sense of purpose was the occupation of the Sud-Aviation works in Nantes. The workers, by 'imitating the students', were rediscovering a form of action that they had far too long discarded while playing the parliamentary game of the reformists and Stalinists ... on 20 May, even the most apathetic joined in, the Citröen works were occupied and a host of others followed suit soon afterwards. Recourse to direct action changed the whole tenor of the struggle, for the workers' self-confidence is enormously increased once they act without delegating any of their power to political parties or trade unions (*Obsolete Communism*, 67).

A similar definition of 'direct action' was given by Bill Haywood of the Industrial Workers of the World in testimony given to the Industrial Relations Commission in 1915. Haywood states that his goal—

working class control of industry—cannot be achieved by political action:

> *Commissioner O'Connell*: 'Have you in mind some other method by
> which it can?'
> *Mr Haywood*: 'Yes sir; I think it can be done by direct action.
> I mean by the organization of the forces of labour' (in Lynd (ed.),
> *Nonviolence in America*, 225).

Direct action is relevant not only to the final aim of seizing power in
industry, but as a method of improving conditions. Haywood comments
about the United Mine Workers:

> They can compel the introduction of safety appliances, of ventilation
> systems, and save in that way thousands of lives every year. . . . If
> they have the power to bring that about by direct action, they have
> the power to reduce their hours; they have the power to increase
> or at least to better the laboring conditions round the mines and
> have better houses (ibid., 226).

The miners in their fight for better conditions sometimes resorted to
direct action, as did civil rights demonstrators later, in order to try to
enforce the existing laws. Haywood described before the Commission the
Cripple Creek strike of 1903 in sympathy with the men working in the
mills of Colorado city, who had gone on strike to enforce the Colorado
state law guaranteeing an eight-hour day. After its formation in 1905 the
IWW soon got involved in action to promote the right to free speech, by
speaking in front of employment agencies in Spokane. The authorities
threw between five and six hundred men and women into jail. The
following year came the Fresno, California, free speech fight. Haywood
comments: 'There the authorities started to arrest men merely for speaking on the street corner, not causing a congestion of traffic' (ibid., 222).

The 'Wobblies' used direct action at times to enforce existing laws, at
times in defiance of immediate rules or authorities but on behalf of
broader constitution principles, and at times to gain limited reforms.
They aimed to use it eventually to usher in revolution. Cole and Postgate
comment on the development of syndicalism in Britain prior to the First
World War:

> Within the ranks of the working class, unparliamentary action
> remained an aspiration. No actual revolutionary movement took
> place; the destructive tendencies of Direct Actionists were expressed
> solely in strikes and sabotage.

> The new philosophy was called Syndicalism or industrial unionism,
> two names with much the same meaning, but the first indicating a
> French inspiration and the second an American.

> The boycott, the sympathetic strike, no peace with the employers,

the smashing of the old reactionary Unions, the breaking of all agreements when convenient, the forcing of non-unionists out of existence, the use of sabotage—all of these principles were taken over in theory from the IWW, but their application was much milder and the enemies far less savage (*The Common People*, 481–2).

Rudolph Rocker in his analysis of anarcho-syndicalism comments that direct action is the only method which has been able to achieve political results:

And the bourgeoisie in its struggles against absolutism has also made abundant use of this method, and by refusal to pay taxes, by boycott and revolution, has defiantly asserted its position as the dominant class in society.

By direct action the Anarcho-Syndicalists mean every method of immediate warfare by the workers against their economic and political oppressors. Among these the outstanding are: the strike, in all its gradations from the simple wage-struggle to the general strike; the boycott; sabotage in its countless forms; anti-militarist propaganda; and in peculiarly critical cases, such, for example, as that in Spain to-day [1930s], armed resistance of the people for the protection of life and liberty (*Anarcho-Syndicalism*, 136).

What Rocker means by sabotage is not, however, primarily the destruction of property. He comments that: 'The term itself is derived from the French word *sabot*, wooden shoe, and means *to work clumsily as if by sabot blows*.' He cites the policy of 'ca'canny' (go slow) as the first and most effective form of sabotage, and also gives the example of the 'grève perlée' by the railway workers of France and Italy—who delayed all the trains by working to rule. He also links sabotage with the sit-down strike inside factories, and the related opportunity to put the machines out of order. In the conception of direct action adopted in this book, sabotage is a borderline case, depending on the context and the aim. Armed insurrection, however, involves a quite different level and type of struggle, and it would be unnecessarily confusing to equate it with direct action.

Gandhian non-violent action

The ethos of Gandhian non-violence is far removed from the class struggle of syndicalism, but when translated into more secularized and militant modes 'non-violent action' is not necessarily very different from the syndicalist concept of direct action. In the American civil rights struggle the initial phase of the movement was marked by conscious adherence to Gandhian philosophy, which was allied to Christian belief. Martin Luther King, who became the leader of the 1955–6 Montgomery Bus Boycott, wrote in *Stride Towards Freedom*:

I became deeply fascinated by his [Gandhi's] campaigns of
non-violent resistance. I was particularly moved by the Salt March to
the Sea and his numerous fasts. . . . I came to feel that this was the
only morally and practically sound method open to oppressed people
in their struggle for freedom (90–1).

In his writings of 1963, *Why We Can't Wait*, King observed:

Nonviolent direct action did not originate in America, but it found
its natural home in this land, where refusal to cooperate with
injustice was an ancient and honorable tradition and where Christian
forgiveness was written into the minds and hearts of good men.
Tested in Montgomery during the winter of 1955–56, and
toughened throughout the South in the eight ensuing years,
nonviolent resistance had become, by 1963, the logical force in the
greatest mass-action crusade for freedom that had ever occurred in
American history (25).

Before 1963 the impetus of the civil rights movement had, however,
already shifted from King's Southern Christian Leadership Conference—
the SCLC—to the more pragmatic, more impatient and inventive student
movement loosely co-ordinated by the Student Non-violent Co-ordinating
Committee—the SNCC. This movement started with the sit-in on 1
February 1960 in Greensboro', North Carolina. The sit-ins spread to
sixty other cities. Howard Zinn comments in *SNCC : The New Abolitionists*:

The sit-ins represented an intricate union of economic and moral
power. To the store owner, they meant a disruption of normal
business; liberal and moderate people in the city and in the nation
now, perhaps for the first time, faced their own status as a
privileged group in American society (28).

The type of action embodied in the sit-in was rapidly extended to attack
segregation in other places. There were 'read-ins' at libraries, 'kneel-ins'
at churches, 'walk-ins' at parks and theatres and 'wade-ins' at swimming
pools and beaches.

The next dramatic move in the civil rights struggle was the use of
direct action to challenge the segregation of facilities at the terminals of
interstate buses—the 1961 'freedom rides'. The original freedom ride
took place in 1947, a year after the Supreme Court decision prohibiting
segregation in interstate travel. The 1961 rides also came after a Supreme
Court decision the previous year—this time outlawing segregation in
restaurants, waiting rooms and other facilities at terminals. Thirteen
freedom riders set out on 4 May to journey from Washington, DC, to
New Orleans. In South Carolina the group were greeted by mob violence.

Really serious violence occurred on 14 May when their bus was set on fire by a mob near Anniston, Alabama, and when on their arrival in Birmingham they were savagely beaten. Students trying to carry on with the ride were assaulted on arriving in Montgomery and were escorted by National Guardsmen to Jackson, Mississippi, where they were arrested. Volunteers arrived in Jackson for the next three months in a campaign to fill the Mississippi jails.

In the summer of 1961 one wing of the SNCC was created to concentrate on registering negro voters, and in August a registration campaign started in McComb, Mississippi. But voter-registration sometimes merged into direct action, as in Selma, Alabama, when the people lining up to register were demonstrating their defiance before the press cameras, and were beaten up and arrested by the police. Part of the campaign for registering voters was the use of mass marches, designed in Arthur Waskow's assessment for: 'mobilizing Negro strength, destroying the old white images of Negro passivity, demonstrating Negro solidarity both to the Negroes themselves and to local white power structures, and attracting national attention both to their old plight and their new militance' (*From Race Riot to Sit-In*, 232). Many Southern police chiefs decided these orderly marches were illegal—as Eugene 'Bull' Connor did during the 1963 campaign in Birmingham.

The Birmingham campaign combined the sit-in tactics to desegregate public places with an economic campaign designed to stop discrimination in the employment of negroes. Bayard Rustin commented:

> The response to Birmingham has been immediate and spontaneous. City after city has come into the fight, from Jackson, Mississippi, to Chesterton, Maryland. The militancy has spread to Philadelphia, where the 'city fathers' and the trade-union movement have been forced to make reluctant concessions. . . . Before Birmingham, the great struggles had been for specific, limited goals. . . . The package deal is the new demand (in Goodman (ed.), *Seeds of Liberation*, 318).

The Birmingham campaign, which brought school children into the struggle and dramatized the brutality of the white power structure through the unrestrained violence of the police, was the climax of non-violent direct action and Luther King's last major success.

Extension of direct action methods to the North was tried, and made some impact. The methods included school boycotts to end *de facto* segregation in schools; and rent strikes by tenants in slum houses. Consumer boycotts were also organized against firms which discriminated against negroes in employment—for example, against Sears Roebuck in 1962; and the Congress of Racial Equality (CORE) experimented with direct obstruction on work sites in protest against the highly discriminatory building trade. A more direct challenge to the government was tried through blockades of council meetings, sit-ins at governmental offices, and 'stall-ins' of traffic by sit-downs on roads and bridges. Waskow comments that 'the tactic of social disruption is much more radical than the other techniques of creative disorder. . . . For what disruption essentially does is challenge the entire society as a racially discriminatory *system*' (*From Race Riot to Sit-In*, 246). But the general verdict by many inside and outside the civil rights movement was that direct action was inadequate to deal with the problems of the Northern slums, rooted as they were, not in the anachronistic, openly colonial attitudes of the South, but in the government of the cities and the nature of the American economy. Anger and despair in the ghetto slums erupted in the riots of the summer of 1965.

Peace movement

During the period in which non-violent action was the accepted tactic of the civil rights movement, it was also adopted as part of the movement against the H-bomb in Britain and the United States. Non-violent direct action meant picketing nuclear research stations, blocking missile bases, trespassing on to air bases and trying to block or board Polaris submarines. A number of attempts were made to enter nuclear testing areas, ranging from the voyage of the *Golden Rule* towards the Eniwetok H-bomb-testing zone in the Pacific in 1958 to the repeated efforts of an international team in 1960 to enter the French Sahara atom site via French West Africa. In the United States non-co-operation was extended to tax refusal and refusal to take part in compulsory civil defence exercises. Annual protests against these exercises in New York started in 1955 when a dozen people refused to take shelter. In 1960 numbers had grown to a thousand, and a number of jail sentences were awarded to the protesters.

The tone and style of these protests tended to stress non-violence, open breaking of the law and willingness to go to jail. The Direct Action Committee in Britain also tried to promote trade union action in the form of token strikes and blacking work on nuclear bases and bomb production. The Committee of 100, which succeeded it, tried to extend the trade union ethos to its own civil disobedience demonstrations, which were based on the idea of mass solidarity and collective responsibility. The first Committee of 100 demonstrations were planned as mass sit-downs in front of government offices in London, and could be seen as a move towards social disruption and a direct challenge to the authorities. The Committee of 100 was less influenced by Gandhian non-violence, and more receptive to anarchist and syndicalist ideas.

The guerrilla image

The idea of non-violent direct action was discredited among those sections of the movement against the war in Vietnam which switched their emphasis from demanding peace to supporting the victory of the National Liberation Front. There were other reasons for this switch of allegiance, in particular among students, from non-violence to violence. In the civil rights campaign the relative success of non-violent action in challenging Southern segregation was not repeated in the Northern ghettos, despite efforts to adapt action tactics to the city slums. The quick governmental response to the riots which erupted in the summer of 1965 also encouraged a black militancy which turned in part to violence as an instrument of social change. Spokesmen for black Americans had also begun to challenge publicly the goal of integration in a white American society—the goal of the sit-ins and freedom rides—and to question the values and nature of that society; a process hastened by the Vietnam war. But the symbolic figure of the Asian, Latin American or African guerrilla was central to the romantic rhetoric, though not to the political thesis of 'Black Power'. Stokeley Carmichael said at the Dialectics of Liberation Conference in London:

> It is the young bloods who contain especially the hatred Che
> Guevara speaks of when he says, and I quote: 'Hatred as an element
> of the struggle, relentless hatred of the enemy that impels us over
> and beyond the natural limitations of man, and transforms us into
> effective, violent, selected and cold killing machines' (in Cooper
> (ed.), *The Dialectics of Liberation*, 162).

The identification of the black minority in the United States with successful guerrilla movements in the Third World, and especially those challenging directly or indirectly the dominance of the United States, is readily understandable. What is more interesting is that young white radicals also imported their belief in violence from the non-European world, just as the previous generation had adopted the non-violence primarily associated with Gandhi. Gareth Stedman Jones, a spokesman for the New Left standpoint, remarks in the course of an article on the development of the student movement:

> In France, Germany and the USA, identification with the example
> of the Vietnamese and Cubans resulted in an early awareness that
> in certain situations the use of nonviolence is tantamount to political
> passivity. This has been reflected in the increasingly militant nature
> of students' demonstrations in many parts of the advanced world—
> itself a reaction to the unremitting violence of US imperialism (in
> Cockburn and Blackburn (eds), *Student Power*, 44).

Student protest

The immediate political associations of direct action in the West today link it to student protest. Colin Crouch begins his book on *The Student Revolt* as follows:

> If a revolutionary student in Britain is asked to say why he protests, why he uses direct action, . . . he is likely to answer in terms that have very little to do with the university as such. . . . He may also tell how the movement for direct action has developed since the Campaign for Nuclear Disarmament made its first limping, liberal gestures towards the politics of the street, and how the idea has been developed from there to involve a theory of the use of direct action, the occupation of factories and universities, as the only relevant political activity at the present time (15).

In the LSE context, direct action came to mean boycotting lectures and classes, sitting-in, and (eventually) tearing down the gates erected by the administration. The evolution of the conflict between militant students and the college authorities showed that the tactic could be seen in two distinct ways by 'moderates' and 'militants' among the students. The difference existed 'between those who sought to use legal, bureaucratic channels as much as possible, using direct action purely as an instrumental political lever of last resort, and those who sought to create a protest movement rooted in the use of direct action as the only valid means of political procedure' (ibid., 52).

Crouch suggests that the tendency towards physical confrontation and violence is a way of symbolizing students' rejection of constitutional and formal politics, and their desire to break out of institutionalized modes of activity and to challenge the whole political system. Crouch is a comparatively hostile, though perceptive, analyst of the student movement in Britain at the end of the 1960s. But his emphasis on the link between direct action and violence is partly confirmed by the statements of the New Left. Stedman Jones, in the article already quoted in *Student Power*, comments that:

> A second legacy of CND was an incomprehension of the necessity of violence in certain political circumstances. CND was inspired by the non-violent dissent of Gandhi, it thereby mistook a tactic for a principle. Such tremendously effective campaigns as that launched by the SDS against the Springer Press in Germany were completely outside the orbit of its conceptions (in Cockburn and Blackburn (eds), *Student Power*, 44).

In the early stages of the conflict between students and the authorities in West Germany, however, the main violence deployed was by the police. It was police violence which helped to consolidate and radicalize a nationwide movement among the students. On 2 June 1967 several thousand West German students demonstrating against the repressive regime of the Shah of Iran congregated outside the Opera House in Berlin where the Shah, who was on an official visit, was to see *The Magic Flute*. As soon as the Shah had entered the Opera House police charged the demonstrators; as a result, twenty students were taken to hospital with injuries and one, Benno Ohnesorg, was shot in the back of the head. A nurse who went to his aid was clubbed by the police. A silent march for Ohnesorg next day was also broken up by the police; and later a ban on demonstrations was announced. Whilst the liberal newspaper, the *Frankfurter Rundschau*, criticized 'the unbelievable brutality' of the police, most West Berlin and West German papers attacked the students, and blamed them for Ohnesorg's death.

After the shooting of the New Left student spokesman Rudi Dutschke in April 1968 by a right-wing fanatic, the students, who attributed this act largely to the role of the mass media in stirring up hatred against student activists, converged on offices of the Springer Press all over the country. Springer, who controlled 90 per cent of the national circulation of Sunday newspapers and 40 per cent of the national daily press, had conducted a sustained and virulent campaign against the students. In Munich students sacked the Springer offices, police and demonstrators fought with stones, and a student and press photographer were killed. But where demonstrations were deliberately non-violent the police also responded with ferocity. A peaceful blockade of the *Bild* office in Frankfurt was according to the *Frankfurter Rundschau* met by the police with water cannons, dogs, tear gas and clubs.

Police brutality began to provoke a somewhat wider opposition among academics, intellectuals and trade unionists—some trade union branches decided as a protest to stop encouraging their members to work in Berlin. A few policemen themselves indicated dissent—twelve told the *Berliner Extra Dienst* that they disagreed with police methods. The president of police in Cologne refused to suppress student demonstrations.

F. C. Hunnius comments in his pamphlet on the SDS use of the shock tactics of direct action and disruption of existing institutions:

> They have learned from their previous 'theoretical phase' that memoranda and petitions do not bring about change, and do not even gain the attention of the public or the governing institutions. As Dutschke has said more than once: 'Only provocation will gain attention' (*Student Revolts*, 27).

But their very success in provocation tended to isolate the students further from the majority of the population.

They did, however, break briefly out of this isolation in a campaign in 1968 which united the Extra-Parliamentary Opposition—a final attempt to defeat the proposed emergency laws which gave the government powers in times of external attack or 'internal danger' to conscript men and women, waive individual liberties, and restrict the role of parliament. Tactics of direct action were integrated into a wider and more orthodox campaign by the left against these laws. In Frankfurt 10,000 workers took part in a short token strike whilst students sealed off the university and held a 'teach-in' at the entrance. On 11 May some 50,000 people converged in a march on Bonn.

The German student movement was marked by political and theoretical seriousness, appropriate to a country in the front line of the cold war, and to German cultural traditions. The theoretical basis of the movement was provided by a humanist interpretation of Marxism. The ethos of the SDS was in clear contrast to the student movements in the United States and Britain, where anarchist and underground influences were often strong—though these influences later took root in Berlin, where the anarchistic 'Kommune K' was founded, and where, according to the *International Times*, by spring 1969 'the dope revolution' was well under way. In Paris in May 1968 the anarchist and 'Hippy' elements of the student rebellion gave the May days their particular stamp. Whilst the battles of the barricades provided genuine drama, and the occupation of the factories major political significance, it was the ideal of *imagination au pouvoir* which endowed May 1968 with a special fascination after the barricades were dismantled, management back in the factories, and the Gaullists returned to power by a striking electoral majority. The May 'events' could be seen as a signal for a new revolutionary era, and they provided material for much political and theoretical analysis of developments in western society. But they were also a symbol of a distinctively new style of protest, which is consciously a youth protest, and which (despite certain conscious borrowings from other cultures and other periods) is distinctive of modern western industrialized societies. It is a style of protest which exists where the beat poets, the Hippies, the drug scene and pop culture move into the arena of politics.

The politics of the counter-culture

One of the early political manifestations within hippy culture was the appearance in the autumn of 1966 of the 'Diggers' in the Haight-Ashbury district of San Francisco. The Diggers began to distribute free food—the food was collected from individual gifts and surpluses of the local markets. They later got hold of two farms, and the following April founded a Black Man's Free Store in the ghetto. The Diggers wrote to the city authorities suggesting they should set up free storehouses. In 1968 *The Diggers' Papers* (reproduced in Peter Buckman's *The Limits of Protest*) set out detailed proposals for free cities within the existing urban environment.

Another early expression of a fusion between underground culture and leftist politics were the Provos of Amsterdam, who roused attention both with their protests and their constructive forms of direct action. The movement began in April 1965 and was anarchist in inspiration, but with a strong beat and artistic element. They claimed to be a 'provotariat' to replace the former proletariat. Its most notorious protest was against the marriage of Princess Beatrix to a German diplomat said to be a former Nazi. The Provos threatened to emit laughing gas from the church organ and reproduce the sound of machine gun fire from hidden loudspeakers. In fact they exploded smoke-bombs on the route of the bridal pair. But their main emphasis was on direct action to improve life in cities, directed particularly against cars. They dramatized their alternative to private cars in their white bike scheme; thirty bicycles were painted white and left round Amsterdam for communal use. The police confiscated them to prevent them being stolen—there is a law in Amsterdam that bicycles on the street should be locked. *Anarchy* commented: 'The White Bikes project is thus a "happening" or improvised drama or a morality play, acted out in the streets of Amsterdam to inculcate a moral lesson, with a beautiful economy of means. But it is also a practical solution to an existing problem' (no. 66, 228).

The Provos' programme included white chimneys—smokeless zones; and white houses—urging families and students to move into and repair condemned houses. They also made proposals for disarming the Dutch police and for clinics providing free contraception and abortion. As a result of Provo provocation the mayor and the city police chief were sacked, and the Provos won a seat on the city council. The Provos soon disbanded their formal organization, and were succeeded by the 'Kabouters' who created their 'Orange Free State' in 1970, with its own economy and welfare bodies and 'army of responsible dissenters'.

Another political grouping grew out of the Hippies, taking over some of the ideas of the Diggers and the joking provocation of the Provos: the 'Yippies' (Youth International Party). They distributed free dollar bills from the gallery of the stock exchange; turned up before the House UnAmerican Activities Committee dressed up in guises ranging from a guerrilla outfit to Father Christmas; nominated a pig for President in the 1968 election; and held a ceremony to levitate the Pentagon as part of the 1967 anti-Vietnam war demonstration in Washington.

Before the Chicago Democratic Convention, the Yippies told the press that they would hold a Festival of Life which would include collecting money in barrels to buy food for everyone, burning 100,000 draft cards, a mass 'stall-in' of vintage cars on the streets, the use of Yippie girls to seduce delegates and dose them with LSD, and bombarding the Convention with mortar fire. According to Abbie Hoffman, their presence at the Convention was: 'an advertisement for revolution. We were a high degree of involvement played out against the dull field of establishment rhetoric' (in Neville, *Play Power*, 56). Whereas the Dutch Provos concentrated mainly on developing forms of direct action, and later on using the existing channels of local politics to promote their programmes, the Yippie style tended towards exploiting the publicity opportunities afforded by the mass media, and staging 'happenings' for their own sake. They expanded the theatrical element in direct action but discarded the practical relevance usually inherent in the method.

The politics of the counter-culture and of the under-thirty generation is, in its associations with pot, long hair, pop and sex, a long way from the concerns of the staid and older generation, and especially perhaps from the respectable working class. But there are, nevertheless, points of contact with the traditional 'proletariat'. The Diggers in America made a link with the poorest and most discriminated against section of American society when they moved into the black ghetto, and the Yippies did the same in a temporary alliance with the Black Panthers. The Provos succeeded in attracting many people with no prior commitment to revolution when they won seats on the city council. There is also a thematic link between the Diggers' and Provos' programmes and sporadic instances of direct actions by housewives and workers, which lies in a common concern about the urban environment—traffic, pollution and homes.

Popular direct action

One of the main targets of spontaneous and local direct action in Britain has been dangerous traffic on the roads. On 8 August 1970 there was a protest which halted the traffic in the Norfolk town of Thetford. According to the *Eastern Daily Press*:

> Waving banners and chanting 'We want a crossing' the mothers, their children, and a growing number of men, walked round in a large circle in the middle of the road, their chants mingling with the car horns of angry drivers held up in a mile-long queue in each direction (quoted in *Peace News*, 14 August 1970, 1).

The protest was sparked off by the death of a fifteen-year-old girl, and was typical of a number of attempts to get local councils to take action to increase road safety. Harold Priestly in his *Voice of Protest* quotes as an example five hundred villagers of Redbourn in Hertfordshire, who on 30 October 1967, walked to and fro over the zebra crossing in the High Street while traffic piled up on both sides, because they wanted a controlled crossing that could be worked from the kerb (7). In November 1971 five hundred people in Cambridge organized a 'bike-in' to protest against traffic. In May 1972 a woman was taken to court for going out in the middle of the night and painting a zebra crossing where the council had failed to provide one.

Environmentalist groups have staged a number of direct action propaganda activities to advertise their cause. For example, the Earth Day plans in New York in April 1970 included free chest X-rays in Manhattan and the dumping of thousands of bottles and tins outside soft drink and beer factories; Friends of the Earth in Britain also dumped 1,500 Schweppes bottles on the doorstep of the company in November 1971. But more relevant is the type of sustained campaign against pollution by local residents which took place in the Port Tennant area of Swansea in 1971. This action was directed against the United Carbon Black factory which emitted clouds of black smuts and dirt that fell on the surrounding houses and streets. Years of representation to the local council brought no relief—and a promise by the factory the previous year to install a new burner did not reduce the dirt. At the end of January a local meeting decided to block the road until the factory stopped spreading smuts. At the beginning of February fifty housewives went onto the road in front of the factory and started turning away traffic to the firm. Shifts of fifty at a time were maintained for three weeks. In the evenings the men returning from work took over. A tent was pitched in the road and fires built. Local traders showed sympathy and brought food. After three weeks several departments of the factory had closed down, and the management negotiated a compromise agreement with the demonstrators, promising to spend £200,000 on pollution control and to stop production when easterly winds were blowing (*Solidarity*, vol. 6, no. 10).

An interesting example of spontaneous local direct action was the campaign by the wives of Hull trawlermen in 1968 after a trawling disaster in which a ship was lost, and it was revealed that the ship had no radio operator on board. Mrs Lilian Bilocca said at the launching of a protest petition: 'If ever I hear about a trawler going to sea without a full complement of crew or without a radio operator, I shall go aboard and wild horses will not drag me off until the ship is properly manned.' Two days later three women tried to leap aboard a trawler about to sail without an operator, and struggled with police. The crews themselves also began to agitate. On 2 and 3 February crews refused to sail because they said that, among other faults, the life jackets were unsafe. Three days later another trawler returned to port after a dispute about the alarm in the crew's quarters. On 14 February it was announced that four inquiries were to be held into the Hull trawler disasters, including one to look into safety measures, pay and hours of work. Tony Topham in a pamphlet on the subject commented:

At the mass meetings of wives and mothers which have been held in Hull, the debate about *how* to achieve results has reproduced, in microcosm, all the historic strategies of the Labour movement, from Fabianism to syndicalism. Frustration over delays and red tape, anger and grief, have brought forth determined advocates of direct action. Mrs Bilocca, leader of much of the agitation, has proved her point that direct action can be made to pay (*Anarchy*, no. 86, 105).

The issue which has in Britain roused widespread effective direct action campaigns is that of homelessness. The most important campaign took place immediately after the Second World War, in the Squatters Movement of 1946. The first phase occurred in the summer of 1945, when a group composed largely of ex-servicemen moved homeless families into empty property during the night in southern seaside resorts, where many large houses were empty except when let out to holiday makers. As a result the government invested local authorities with wider powers to requisition houses. The main thrust of the Squatters Movement the following year was to occupy empty army and airforce barracks and camps. The first family spontaneously took the initiative at Scunthorpe in Lincolnshire in May. By October according to the government's own figures, 39,535 people were squatting in 1,038 camps. The Ministry of Works offered Aneurin Bevan 850 former service camps 'to help him in his emergency housing drive'.

A member of the Squatters Movement records that:

> As the camps began to fill, the squatters turned to other empty buildings: houses, shops, mansions, disused school buildings, race tracks and a stadium, were among the places occupied, and on August 26 two Aberdeen hotels and a hostel were taken . . . the final and most spectacular phase of the campaign began in London on Sunday the 8th September, when the 148 luxury flats of Duchess of Bedford House, Kensington, another block in Weymouth Street, Marylebone, and houses in Holland Park and Campden Hill, were invaded (*Anarchy*, no. 23, 10–11).

Squatting was revived again, though on a much smaller scale, in the late 1960s. The first stage of the campaign revolved round a hostel for homeless families owned by the Kent County Council at West Malling, Kent. Some of the families themselves rebelled against a system which separated husbands from their wives, and only allowed them to visit during certain hours. After a campaign which included deliberate defiance by the husbands of the hostel regulations and of the court injunctions designed to make them obey the rules, and sustained picketing of the chief welfare officer, Kent County Council gave way.

The London Squatting Campaign was formed in November 1968. Jim Radford wrote in an article early in 1969:

> On December 1st we invaded the Hollies, a luxury block in East London, where many of the flats have remained empty since the building was completed four years ago. This was a token

demonstration for the purpose of drawing public attention to a major social evil. On December 21st we went a step further. Together with a number of homeless families we took over the Old Vicarage in Capworth Street, E 11, a substantial twenty-four roomed house that has been empty ever since the vicar moved . . . three years ago (*Anarchy*, no. 97, 80).

Families in Notting Hill and in Ilford took over houses in January and February and more squatters groups were formed. Some councils tried evictions and court injunctions to stop squatting; but in many cases squatters and councils came to an agreement, and squatters were allowed to remain. For example, the *Guardian* reported on 18 March 1970 that: 'Squatting, Lewisham style, has become "respectable" . . . the squatters now have 30 families installed in houses that would otherwise be empty awaiting redevelopment' (1). The Squatting Association took responsibility for moving families out when redevelopment started, and for collecting low rents for the occupied houses.

Direct action centred on housing problems has not, however, been confined to the occupation of empty houses. In 1971 the Southwark Family Squatters Association barricaded themselves in at the town hall. A vigorous campaign was also undertaken to get tenants living in flats intolerably close to a new motorway rehoused. A *Guardian* article on 7 August 1970 reflected that:

> If you want to win the battle of homes versus motorways there
> appears to be no substitute for proletarian militancy. That seems to
> be the sad lesson brought home to the inhabitants of Gilda Court,
> a genteel decaying block of owner-occupied flats . . . there seems
> little hope that they will be rehoused with the alacrity shown by the
> Greater London Council towards some of its tenants affected by the
> Westway motorway.
>
> In the latter case the Walmer Road Action Committee's
> militancy is by no means abated. They complain that the GLC has
> committed itself only to rehouse the tenants of eight houses whereas
> 30 houses had been made uninhabitable. . . . If no satisfactory
> decision was forthcoming from the GLC by today there would be
> a 'massive' campaign to disrupt traffic (5).

The tendency to resort to direct action to protect one's rights has extended to the factory floor. Faced with the threat of redundancy, in a wider context of high levels of unemployment, workers in a number of firms began in 1971 and 1972 to adopt methods more militant, and more appropriate, than the normal strike. The first and most significant action was that taken by shop stewards and workers in the yards of the Upper Clyde Shipbuilders, who, faced with the prospect of the yards being closed down, organized a 'work-in', and took over control from the management. The work-in, prolonged over several months, was successful in getting the government to reverse its declared policy of not giving further financial aid to maintain the yards, though the workers had to accept compromises. The militancy of the Upper Clyde workers lay, however, more in their methods than in their long-term goals. Workers' control was used as a tactic, but not promoted as an aim.

The example of the UCS workers was followed at a number of other factories. A sit-in at the Plessey Electronics factory in Dunbartonshire began on 3 September 1971, when all the workers there had received redundancy notices. The workers took over control of the gates and refused to let machinery be moved in or out. Workers in Plessey's four factories in Ilford promised to 'black' all machinery and materials from the Dunbartonshire factory. On 4 January 1972, 150 workers at an engineering factory at Mold, North Wales, took it over to prevent its closure. The gate was manned by shifts of about thirty men. Two days later a sit-in took place at the Fisher-Bendix electrical factory in Liverpool to stop the owners closing down the factory. Shop stewards reported that the management agreed to leave the factory immediately after the meeting which decided on the occupation of the factory. A more unusual example of militancy was provided by twelve women who staged a sit-in at a factory at Norfolk at the end of March 1971, and started to canvass orders for leather shoulder bags and skirts to keep the factory open. A *New Statesman* article on 28 April 1972, on a series of sit-ins in Manchester, commented:

> There are at present approximately 30 sit-ins in progress throughout the country and more are likely. And for the first time they are nearly all factory sit-ins. . . . Now in Manchester a wave of lock-outs has been countered by a wave of factory occupations (549).

Whilst these tactics may be seen in part as an indication of a new militancy among industrial workers in Britain, they also reflect the prevalence of direct action as a method used both by movements committed to an ideological goal—for example, the campaign by Welsh Nationalists for use of the Welsh language—and by groups seeking redress for more immediate grievances. The *Guardian* reported, for example, on 26 May 1972, that 'More than 300 prisoners staged what the Home Office described as "a quiet, good-humoured sit-down demonstration" at Walton Prison, Liverpool, yesterday. Similar sit-downs have been staged in other prisons this week.' Other prisoners at Walton jail were said to be on hunger strike against prison conditions.

The relative respectability, as well as the prevalence, of the sit-in tactic is indicated by the fact that in September 1971, French police unions were threatening to occupy the Ministry of Finance and M. Chaban-

Delmas's official residence if the prime minister would not listen to their grievances on pay and bad working conditions.

In trying to justify the direct action tactics used to stop the all-white South African cricket team touring Britain in 1970 Peter Hain appeals to the comparative legitimacy of much popular direct action:

> By attempting to stop the matches, we were accused of 'infringing on people's lawful rights to watch cricket and rugby'. This may have been true and, taken out of the context of the issue at stake, sounds plausible. The fact that people's 'lawful rights' are just as often 'infringed' by militant farmers driving tractors through towns, by industrial strikes and by disruptions of traffic by mothers demanding a zebra crossing, is conveniently forgotten (*Don't Play with Apartheid*, 200).

Nature of direct action

Local direct action on issues like housing may be widely (though not totally) accepted as a valid means of breaking through bureaucratic inertia, and as a form of protest which can be institutionalized and accommodated in the existing organization of local and national government. But a number of elements in direct action are often seen as a challenge to parliamentary liberalism, particularly when direct action is allied to the rhetoric of guerrilla warfare and the declared intent to challenge the public order with disruptive violence. In defining direct action it is important to distinguish between the real and the metaphorical elements in the guerrilla image. Armed and systematic violence against government agents—army and police—or against sections of the population falls into the category of guerrilla warfare proper. Hence some minority groups which have developed out of the student movement, and which have become committed to the use of bombs and to shooting the police, like the 'Weathermen' underground in the United States and the 'Baader-Meinhof' group in West Germany, have turned to real guerrilla tactics. Methods like political kidnapping and hijacking aeroplanes which rely on use of arms are also much closer to guerrilla warfare than to the usual methods of direct action, and have in practice normally been carried out by guerrilla movements—or else for highly individual reasons, like trying to escape to another country, or to win ransom money.

Sabotage is a borderline area between guerrilla war and direct action, since it may be an adjunct to para-military activities—for example, blowing up bridges, police stations or embassies. But it may also be directly related to a specific direct action campaign, as in industrial sabotage, or burning draft records. It is also a borderline case between violence and non-violence, since destruction of property is quite distinct from physical attacks on people; but use of explosives may accidentally endanger human life even when this is not intended. Moreover, the use of sabotage may encourage the type of organization and ethos conducive to full-scale armed attacks.

The role of violence in direct action is complicated by the possibility of resort to defensive violence. The dividing line between offensive and defensive violence may become blurred—or defensive preparations may be interpreted as evidence of offensive intent (in part the fate of the Black Panthers, whose conspicuous guns provided a rationale for the police to shoot-up their headquarters). But genuine defensive violence does occur, and may be a natural adjunct of direct action. Picket lines which fight back when the police charge them, squatters who barricade themselves in against bailiffs sent to evict them, and civil rights demonstrators who fight off a lynching party are obvious examples. The violence is not an inherent part of picketing, squatting or sit-ins, but it may arise out of these methods of direct action.

It is also necessary to distinguish between direct action and modes of violence which do not fall under the category of guerrilla warfare. Systematic violent clashes between demonstrators and the police or army —a development out of the student movement in Japan in the late 1960s— or resort to street fighting and barricades, as in May 1968, may arise out of marches or direct action demonstrations. But street fighting, or organized assaults on police using weapons like clubs, involves escalation of protest beyond the level of direct action to riot, the barricades, or virtual insurrection. Exact borderlines may be easier to draw in a specific situation than in the abstract—but there is a threshold between spontaneous fighting, or intentional but unorganized scuffling, between demonstrators and police on the one hand, and the highly organized, continuous or dangerous use of violence on the other. The Suffragette raids on the Houses of Parliament, or marches on the American Embassy in Grosvenor Square in London, fall into the former category. The student demonstrations in Paris in May 1968, moved from the first level to the second, initially in response to police action. The student protest in West Germany in the late 1960s, and the civil rights movement in Northern Ireland, tended (after the initial phase of protest) to involve both levels of action at various times.

A further difficulty arises not from the actual methods adopted in a campaign, but the blurred vision we have of the nature of 'violence' in politics. The rhetoric of radicals who identify themselves with guerrilla resistance encourages an exaggerated view of the amount of violence really employed in most direct action demonstrations in western Europe and the United States. Both the press and liberal critics also tend to magnify the physical violence which does occur. In this context it is relevant to recall the degree of 'violence' associated with ordinary election meetings in the nineteenth century—or the aftermath of a football match today. Methods which are primarily obstructive may be labelled arbitrarily as 'violent'—for instance, interrupting a rugby game. Trevor Huddleston commented, in the course of an interview about the proposed interruptions of the South African cricket team's tour in 1970: 'How can it be violence when a bloke runs on a rugby ground and scatters tintacks? This is just direct action' (*The Times*, 29 April 1970, 12).

The image of the guerrilla making some dramatic incursion on to the scene has also become widely used in the context of protest movements, even where the activity in question is totally non-violent, as in the case of 'guerrilla theatre'. In this sense flamboyant, unexpected or disruptive tactics—which are not in essence at all violent—may be covered by the idea of guerrilla action. This borrowing of terminology in part reflects fashion, and in part the lack of suitable descriptive words. Earlier direct action movements have borrowed military terms like 'raid' and 'occupation'; and even marches and pickets are military in origin.

Ideological adherence to either Gandhian or guerrilla warfare theories by practitioners of direct action, and the corresponding rhetoric of non-violent or violent confrontation, has tended to cause confusion. If the various forms of systematic or armed violence are regarded as separate modes of political activity, then the predominant methods of direct action clearly do not *depend* on violence—but they do not require strict adherence to 'non-violence' either. Direct action may be seen as an 'a-violent' approach, which can be given either a violent or non-violent emphasis. Emphasis on non-violence will affect the tone, and may restrict the scope of direct action; but emphasis on violence cannot be taken very far without abandoning direct action altogether in favour of more specifically violent styles of resistance or rebellion.

Although 'direct action' is now particularly associated with the Left, it also has certain connotations which associate it with the far Right. An *Observer* correspondent reported from Bonn on 29 November 1970:

> West Germany's right-wing extremists, exasperated by their
> setbacks in recent elections, are organising themselves for a 'direct
> action' campaign against Chancellor Willy Brandt's Government.
>   To attract public attention they are planning street demonstrations,
> disturbances at official ceremonies and the disruption of meetings
> addressed by Government leaders. . . . Undercover agents inside the
> 90 odd organisations of the extremist right-wing fringe report an
> increasing willingness among their members to resort to violence. . . .
> The recent sharp increase of anonymous threats received by
> Cabinet Ministers is seen as a reflection of this new mood (8).

Twenty years earlier members of the Poujadist Movement were trying to prevent others paying their taxes and to hinder officials collecting taxes. William Kornhauser in his study *The Politics of Mass Society* describes the methods used by the Poujadists in France and comments 'This is direct action' (45).

The significance of right wing use of direct action can only be understood in relation to the movements involved. In the case of Poujadism, Raymond Aron has suggested that it linked up with the long tradition of French peasant non-co-operation and militant protest. Indeed, in the early 1960s, when the Poujadist movement had declined, Breton farmers were barricading the roads to protest about prices received for their crops. Four thousand young farmers drove their tractors into a market town in north Finistère in June 1961, and took over the sub-prefecture. After two of their leaders were arrested, roads were blockaded in sympathy and farmers demonstrated throughout the west of France. But according to John Ardagh's account: 'For the first time French farmers were demonstrating *for* progress instead of against it' (*The New France*, 119). Forms of non-co-operation and of sometimes violent resistance have frequently been used to express discontent among small farmers—especially in the populist movements in the United States and Canada. This kind of agrarian unrest has led the participants to support both left-and right-wing ideologies; but direct action and disruption by farmers and peasants has never provided the focal point of militancy for a movement espousing a fully fascist ideology.

Fascist movements have, however, often sought at certain stages to identify themselves with popular discontents and to use some of the theoretical and emotional appeals made by the Left. Robert Benewick in his study of the British fascists between the wars records the following incidents:

> The Blackshirts were now receiving their share of publicity. They capitalized on the tithe disputes which were taking place in Suffolk. On three occasions, beginning in the summer of 1933, they appointed themselves the defenders of the downtrodden against the established forces. In one incident the Blackshirts took over a farm near Wortham, Suffolk, without the owner's consent and despite police warnings. They dug trenches, erected barricades, and raised the Fascist flag (*Political Violence and Public Order*, 90–1).

Moreover, in so far as they share the characteristics of an extra-parliamentary opposition appealing direct to 'the people' fascist movements might be expected to use some of the methods of the Left.

Since the connections between direct action and fascism are highly emotive several obvious points need to be made. One is that political methods cannot be judged in isolation from the political goals, ideology and organization of those using them. A fascist party arouses concern even when it confines itself to perfectly legal forms of protest and electoral politics. Second, non-co-operation or disruption is quite distinct from physical intimidation and the resort to armed violence; and if fascist movements link the two, this is due primarily to their prior adherence to violence. This connects with the third point, that although fascist movements have used electoral and direct action tactics, what has typified genuinely fascist movements in the past has been their para-military style and their use of violent intimidation. This was true even of the British Union of Fascists, which made concessions to the parliamentary and liberal emphasis of British political culture. The dangers of direct action for liberal democracy do not spring from its occasional use by fascist or neo-fascist groups, who pose a more fundamental threat to liberalism. The threat to liberal democracy posed by left wing movements who espouse violence is one of the main themes to be explored in this book. But as the examples of direct action given earlier show, there is no necessary connection between the resort to direct action and the resort to violence.

The central methods of direct action comprise, in accordance with the line of analysis adopted here, the tactics evolved within the labour movement—strikes, go-slows and boycotts; and the more recent forms of physical obstruction and intervention—sit-ins and trespassing. A third category is that of civil disobedience: deliberately breaking laws considered unjust, or the laws of a state pursuing unjust or inhuman policies. Another historical form of direct action is non-co-operation with the state, for example, through tax refusal, or in the more radical form of draft resistance and disobedience inside the army. There are many other possible kinds of financial sanction, for example, the idea of a run on the banks, and many ingenious forms of protest on the margin of direct action, like taking out shares in order to disrupt shareholders' meetings. But this summary catalogue of methods indicates the general scope and nature of direct action as defined in this discussion.

Whilst it is necessary to distinguish direct action from guerrilla warfare and street fighting, it is also necessary to mark it off, at the other end of the scale, from political activity relying on speeches, leaflets and general propaganda which are the stock in trade of constitutional pressure groups, and a necessary element in any type of movement. They may well be a prelude to direct action, or an ancillary aspect of a direct action campaign, but they are not in themselves a form of direct action, unless undertaken as a challenge to specific laws or the authorities.

There is a rather indeterminate area, which is on the borderline of direct action, which may be termed symbolic action. This category of protest action includes parades, marches and outdoor rallies designed to demonstrate mass opposition. It also covers vigils, fasts and other modes of expressing individual commitment. Symbolic action may simply be an extension of other forms of propaganda, and a way of exerting public pressure on the government. In a liberal state it will normally be a legal and accepted form of protest. But symbolic demonstrations may signify a tendency to take action beyond the constitutional limits of protest, and they are usually an essential element in the creation of a movement of mass resistance. Rallies, marches and individual acts of symbolic protest may easily be treated as illegal, especially when the authorities are nervous and regard them as acts subversive of public order. They then become a form of direct action.

A number of other criteria are relevant in identifying a model of direct action—for example, it implies organization and a conscious will to resist or to affect policy. Thus the purely religious conscientious objector escapes the category, but a campaign of conscientious objection of the kind organized in Britain in the First World War falls within it. Similarly, the individual deserter who opts out may be doing so for purely personal reasons—but in a context of political agitation inside or outside the army, desertion becomes a form of direct action. Good Soldier Schweik tactics of over-co-operation and playing dumb may also be an individual escape route, or fall into a pattern of indirect obstruction on a mass scale.

Because direct action implies organization it also implies group, if not mass, action. So where individual protest is undertaken it is with the aim of sparking off a wider movement on these lines, or as part of a planned campaign. Except in the rare case where a one-man campaign could succeed, purely individual 'witness' in the Quaker or pacifist tradition does not accord with the aims and ethos of direct action. But at the other extreme, where really mass resistance or rebellion occurs, direct action may give way to insurrection or revolution. Mutiny, like the general strike, is a borderline example. If limited to particular ends, or particular sections of the armed forces, mutiny may be an extreme form of direct action. But if the aims become more ambitious, or numbers increase, it may well be the prologue to revolution.

The distinction between direct action and revolution is not ultimately one of methods—a revolution will probably involve resort to arms, but it is theoretically possible that the government could be overthrown by means of a mutiny and general strike. The crucial distinction concerns the aims and context in which the methods are used. Any movement which results in the overthrow or seizure of governmental power—whether through spontaneous insurrection, organized revolution or a plotted *coup d'état*—has moved into a new dimension of political action distinct from a campaign for limited (if radical) ends within the framework of the existing state. Direct action may however create the conditions for overthrowing the government.

Direct action is primarily a method of protest or resistance. But it often has constructive elements. Homeless families squatting in empty houses, or workers taking over the factories where they work, are not only engaging in physical intervention but are demonstrating in embryo new forms of organization and new social solutions to their grievances. An interesting example is the idea of the 'reverse strike'. In Sicily Danilo Dolci led sixty-five unemployed men to repair a road just outside Partinico. Their aim was to obey Article IV of the Italian Constitution which declares all citizens have a right and a duty to work. The police ordered the demonstrators to stop work and go home. This first protest took place on 15 December 1955. Six weeks later, after a day of fasting to protest against fishing abuses, two hundred men set out to repair the road. Police had banned the action in advance. Dolci and six others were arrested. Direct action demonstrations may also lead to attempts to create new institutions—for instance, the idea of a 'free university' arising out of sit-ins on university campuses.

At its most ambitious level a direct action campaign may entail creating a parallel set of institutions to replace the existing authorities. This stage of a movement may merge into a conscious attempt to overthrow the existing authorities altogether. Syndicalism, which relied on the trade unions to act as the organs of a new society, combined from the start direct action methods of resistance with strengthening of alternative organizational structure. Moreover, for the syndicalist movement strikes had the same effect as direct action demonstrations have sometimes had among students today—not only did they sharpen the struggle against the powers that be, but also the very fact of taking part in action promoted a feeling of solidarity and community.

Many students advocating direct action in the late 1960s saw it as part of a wider movement aiming at direct democracy. There is a natural psychological connection between direct action protests and attempts to create direct democracy, because of the sense of community and spontaneity protests may evoke.

Dave Dellinger wrote about the 1968 confrontation in Chicago:

> The triumph of Chicago was the triumph of street protesters who displayed courage, imagination, flexibility, and fraternal solidarity as they refused to knuckle under to the police. The role of centralized, formal leadership was minimal in these events. A crude but creative kind of participatory democracy was at work. The organic needs of the occasion, the interacting but spontaneous reactions of the participants, set the tone (*Revolutionary Nonviolence*, 399).

A second example arises from the 1946 Squatters Movement referred to earlier. According to the account in *Anarchy*:

> A notable feature of the whole campaign was the way in which, quite spontaneously and without disputes, the accommodation was divided among the would-be squatters in accordance with their

needs, the size of the families, and so on. . . . Communal cooking, laundering and nursery facilities sprang up. Fathers took turns to stoke the boilers, mothers took turns to do the settlement's shopping, and the children collected up the rubbish left by the army and made bonfires of it. . . . One of the remarkable features of the squatters' communities was that they were formed from people who had very little in common except their homelessness—tinkers and university dons were amongst them (no. 23, 12–13).

Community organizing may encompass both direct action and institutions designed to promote direct democracy. The Notting Hill project in London, which started in 1966, has combined constructive efforts to ameliorate local problems, like housing and lack of play space, with pressure on the local authorities and direct action demonstrations. In order to give residents of the Goldborne ward direct representation, an elected neighbourhood council has been integrated into the local government framework.

There is also a theoretically logical connection between direct democracy and direct action, which is a means of bypassing formal institutions and exerting direct individual pressure on policy. It can therefore be seen as one way of practising direct democracy within a parliamentary framework. The degree to which direct action is intended to be a democratic mode of exerting power through individual and mass popular action is directly relevant to its role in a liberal democracy.

2 Direct action in the constitutional tradition

Contemporary movements resorting to direct action and their theoretical sources were examined briefly in the previous chapter. But a description of direct action would be very incomplete without reference to the part direct action has played in winning current constitutional and democratic rights. This point has not been overlooked by theorists of direct action. Rudolph Rocker, for instance, stresses that direct action is not unique to syndicalism:

> Political rights do not originate in parliaments, they are, rather, forced upon parliaments from without. And even their enactment into law has for a long time been no guarantee of their security. . . . Even in those countries where such things as freedom of the press, right of assembly, right of combination, and the like, have long existed, governments are constantly trying to restrict those rights or to reinterpret them by judicial hairsplitting. . . . The peoples owe all the political rights and privileges which we enjoy today in greater or lesser measure . . . to their own strength. . . . Only after the workers had by direct action confronted parliament with accomplished facts, did the government see itself obliged to take the new situation into account and give legal sanction to the trade unions (*Anarcho-Syndicalism*, 130–1).

In examining the role of direct action in previous struggles in Britain to reform parliament, extend the suffrage, secure freedom of the press, and consolidate the right to form trade unions and to strike, it is not always easy to disentangle direct action from constitutional methods, which were in some cases still evolving or of doubtful legality at the time, so that their practice might in itself be a form of direct action. Neither can various forms of non-co-operation and demonstrations of defiance always be easily separated from threatened or actual riots and the possibility of violent revolution in the background. But this ambiguity is intrinsic to the method, and examination of the link between illegal action and popular violence in the past may have a bearing on the link between direct action and violence in the present.

Wilkes and liberty

The role of popular pressure, non-co-operation and disobedience in gaining constitutional liberties is illustrated by the popular agitation which had as its slogan 'Wilkes and Liberty'. This agitation—which included defiance of the government by the City of London, and court rulings sympathetic to Wilkes and his supporters—concerned freedom of the press, the legitimacy of certain current legal practices and the reform of parliament. The Wilkes movement involved a wide range of methods which have since become common forms of protest, and it marked an evolution from sporadic rioting towards organized radical politics. The events are therefore set out in some detail.

The first move was made by the government, which arrested Wilkes in May 1763 for an issue of the paper he edited, the *North Briton*. This issue, which became famous as 'Number 45', attacked King George III's speech to parliament in defence of the peace treaty just reached with France, and alleged that ratification of the treaty had been obtained through bribery. Wilkes was charged with seditious libel, and forty-eight other people were detained and questioned under a 'general warrant' issued by the government. Wilkes was a Member of Parliament at the time and claimed that he should have been protected from arrest by parliamentary privilege. The judge upheld this plea and Wilkes was released. The judge also questioned the use of a general warrant, and when the proof readers and printers claimed damages from the government for wrongful arrest they received substantial compensation. Two years later a ruling by the same judge conclusively labelled the practice of issuing general warrants as illegal.

After initial success, Wilkes suffered a setback. A second charge against him was brought before a judge sympathetic to the government, parliament was prevailed upon to condemn Number 45 and a loyal MP wounded Wilkes in a duel. When Wilkes escaped to Paris he was condemned as an outlaw by the courts for not standing trial, and expelled from parliament. But five years later, in 1768, he returned to London to defy the authorities and become a popular hero. He contested a parliamentary election for London, which he lost, and then ran as a candidate for Middlesex, which he won. Wilkes enjoyed enough support from the 'mob' to choose his own time for surrendering himself to the authorities. There were demonstrations outside his prison, and the military killed seven people whilst dispersing the demonstration, thus turning it into 'the massacre of St George's Fields'.

When Wilkes appeared before the court the judge cancelled his outlawry and sentenced him to only twenty-two months in prison, plus a fine of £1,000. However, in February 1769, the House of Commons expelled Wilkes for an inflammatory denunciation of a government message congratulating the troops responsible for the 'massacre'. His expulsion was met immediately by riots, and began a long struggle between the electorate of Middlesex and the government-controlled parliament. When a new writ was issued for the Middlesex election Wilkes was returned unopposed, but promptly expelled again by parliament. In the third election an opponent was found to stand against Wilkes, but no voters would nominate him. Wilkes was returned and expelled for the third time. In the fourth election the anti-Wilkes candidate managed to secure 296 votes to Wilkes's 1,143. The Commons expelled Wilkes, passed a motion stating his opponent should have been returned, and proceeded to seat the latter. On his release from jail Wilkes became an alderman of the City of London.

Wilkes's last major campaign and greatest achievement was concerned with extending the freedom of the press. Whilst he was alderman of the City of London two London printers were ordered to appear before the House of Commons to answer charges of breach of privilege for printing reports of parliamentary debates. This had been held a breach of privilege since 1738 but from 1768, several papers began to run regular parliamentary reports. The two printers went into hiding, and the Commons, whilst summoning a further six printers, offered a reward for their arrest. When one of them was brought to the Guildhall, Wilkes, who was then the presiding justice, immediately released the printer. When the Commons next sent its own messenger to arrest another printer who had refused to appear before them, both the parliamentary messenger and the printer were taken by a constable to the Guildhall, where the printer was released and the messenger charged with assaulting a freeman of the City of London.

Wilkes and his associates, who had privately encouraged both newspapers and printers in their defiance, had now provoked a full-scale confrontation with parliament and the king, with the power of the City behind the rights of free publication. The Commons demanded that the Lord Mayor and another alderman who had acted with Wilkes at the Guildhall should appear before them. Despite Wilkes's efforts to be summoned himself he was not finally called to appear. But both Alderman Oliver and the Lord Mayor Crosby appeared separately at the Commons, accompanied by enormous crowds of supporters, many wearing badges with the slogan 'Crosby, Wilkes, Oliver and the liberty of the Press'. Both defied parliament and were imprisoned in the Tower, where they became the focus for widespread popular support. They were released when parliament rose, and the printers themselves were never arrested. The newspapers continued to print parliamentary debates, and parliament did not try to dispute their right to do so any further. Wilkes had said in the first issue of the *North Briton*: 'The liberty of the Press is the birthright of a Briton, and is justly esteemed the firmest bulwark of the liberties of this country' (in Williams, *The Long Revolution*, 207). His own campaign, and the later struggle of the 'unstamped' radical press, helped to make these words true.

The Wilkes agitation also helped to promote democratic ideas. In the struggle centring on the Middlesex elections demands that the will of the Middlesex electors should be respected by parliament were extended to a programme calling for the exclusion of pensioners and placemen from the Commons, annual or triennial parliaments, and a fair and equal representation of the people (though this did not mean a radical extension of the franchise). Wilkes was finally seated as member for Middlesex in December 1774, having again been returned unopposed. But once in parliament he did not progress beyond making periodic appeals for reform.

He had, however, created the basis for future democratic campaigns and established the importance of certain methods. G. D. H. Cole and Raymond Postgate comment of the Wilkes organization:

> Their main weapon was the introduction, or at least revival, of
> *public meetings* as a method of expressing opinion and influencing
> the Government. These meetings were called for the purpose,
> generally, of drafting and signing a petition to the King or the
> Commons; they were addressed by itinerant Wilkite speakers. . . .
> Occasional meetings of county freeholders were not unknown,
> though they were unusual except at elections; apart from them,
> this most essential and apparently natural expression of democracy
> had largely disappeared (*The Common People*, 103).

Another important tactic, which sparked off a dispute about the role of a member of parliament in relation to his electors, was the practice of issuing instructions to MPs about how to vote on the Middlesex election question, and asking for pledges on various issues.

But there were also more colourful, and more potentially violent, forms of protest. During the third contested Middlesex election, Wilkes supporters paraded through London before going to vote at Brentford. According to a contemporary account a great body of freeholders marched along Pall Mall, headed by 'a band of music, with colours flying', and stopped in front of the Palace, where the band began to play. 'This alarmed the Guards, who marched out of the gate with their bayonets fixed; but the company marched on peaceably for Brentford' (Rudé, *Wilkes and Liberty*, 69). Another demonstration of three-hundred on horse back rode via the Old Bailey and Fleet Street to Brentford. Wilkes's victory was received with illuminations and the ringing of church bells. When the king went to the races at Epsom the *Gentleman's Magazine* reported that 'a fellow who stood near His Majesty had the audacity to hallow out, "Wilkes and Liberty for ever!" ' (ibid., 71).

During the same period as the height of the Wilkes campaign, though not on the evidence directly connected with it, there was considerable unrest among many London trades. At the beginning of 1768 both the weavers and the coal heavers engaged in protracted and bitter disputes to obtain better pay and conditions. The coal heavers during a riot took up the cry 'Wilkes and coal-heavers for ever'. In May the *Gentleman's*

Magazine noted: 'A great body of sailors assembled at Deptford, forcibly went on board several ships, unreefed the top-sails, and vowed no ships should sail till the merchants had consented to raise their wages' (ibid., 91). In May also the hatters went on strike, 2,000 Thames watermen demonstrated in front of the Mansion House, and 2,000 journeymen tailors alarmed parliament by marching to the House with a petition. But the only link between industrial action and parliamentary reform was the general mood of popular unrest and Wilkes as a symbol of defiance to the authorities. The Wilkes campaign, although it gained support of the 'mob', was not a coherent and genuinely radical movement. It was to be succeeded by movements in which parliamentary reform and the freedom of the press were much more closely linked with the trade union demands of the artisan class.

The struggle for parliamentary reform and extension of the franchise, which culminated in the 1832 Reform Bill, illustrates the importance of mass agitation and of unconstitutional or illegal action. From its inception in the 1770s the movement for reform gained impetus from its more radical adherents, whilst moderate middle-class reformers sometimes used the pressure of extra-parliamentary action and the threat of violent revolt, and sometimes shrank back from the implications of this course. In the 1770s supporters of Burgh, who demanded universal male suffrage, made plans to create a Grand National Association more representative than parliament which would, unless MPs pledged themselves to reform, usurp the role of parliament and act as a legislative body.

In the 1790s the movement for reform was based on numerous local organizations designed to promote radical ideas. These groups met together in two conventions. The forms of organization and action were constitutional. But the threat of lower-class militancy which these bodies represented, and their avowed support for the Jacobin clubs in France, both invited government suppression. Anticipating government action, the second convention made plans for an underground organization. In 1794 the government arrested leading members of the London Corresponding Society and charged them with high treason. The juries refused to condemn the defendants to being hanged, disembowelled and quartered, and resorted to that form of non-co-operation often practised by sympathetic eighteenth-century juries—finding the prisoners 'Not guilty'.

But repression temporarily quashed the movement. The government was aided also by the patriotism engendered by the Napoleonic wars. It was not until 1816 that a new popular movement emerged to support the small group of middle-class reformers based on the Hampden clubs. In August the Prince Regent refused to receive a petition from the Corporation of London. In September a Committee of Public Safety was formed, which promoted a series of mass meetings to endorse a petition to the Prince Regent.

At the first meeting in Spa Fields, orator Henry Hunt addressed a huge crowd flanked by supporters carrying a cap of liberty on the end of a pike and a tricolour flag of the future British Republic. The Regent refused to accept the petition, and as a result a protest meeting was called for 2 December. The Spenceans, a group holding extreme Jacobin views and demanding economic equality, harangued the meeting, and a portion of the crowd then raided a few gunsmiths' shops, marched through the City and made for the Tower. These events followed by an apparent assassination attempt on the Prince Regent panicked the press and parliament, caused respectable leaders of the reform movement to draw back from agitation, and encouraged the government to suspend habeas corpus and pass severe restrictions on holding public meetings.

A rally in Manchester to protest against the suspension of habeas corpus was planned for March 1817. It was followed by a march to London by unemployed weavers, the 'Blanketeers' who were carrying petitions. But the march, which was rumoured to have violent intent, was broken up and the leaders arrested. A second march which really did have revolutionary aims was planned in secret. But the main organizers were arrested in advance. However, when a respected Yorkshire paper revealed that the plot had been promoted by a government agent provocateur, a Yorkshire jury acquitted the accused. In January 1818 parliament, then in a more liberal and relaxed mood, repealed the suspension of habeas corpus.

Protest meetings demanding reform were renewed in 1819. A crowd of between 25,000 and 50,000 met in Birmingham in July, and overcame their lack of representation by electing Sir Charles Wolseley to go to London on their behalf. The government took Sir Charles and other reform leaders to court. Other big cities were deterred from following Birmingham's example. But in Manchester 60,000 people assembled at St Peter's Fields to hear Henry Hunt on 16 August. Cavalry and mounted yeomanry charged the crowd, killed eleven people and wounded about four hundred. While Lord Sidmouth publicly congratulated the Manchester authorities, mass meetings of protest erupted over the 'Massacre of Peterloo'. Henry Hunt, out on bail after his arrest, was greeted in London by a crowd of 200,000. Moderate leaders became active again, and Cobbett returned from voluntary exile in America, bringing an urn holding Tom Paine's ashes. The radical press began to flourish. The government responded with the Six Acts designed to prevent large public meetings, curb the radical press and halt the movement for reform. Partly as a result of the Acts the movement did decline—though during the 1820s editors, printers and distributors of the radical unstamped press challenged the stamp tax and the laws of libel and sedition, in a successful struggle for true freedom of the press.

The next period of mass agitation for reform occurred in 1831–2, when the reformers drew on constitutional measures of protest—mass meetings and petitions, and on non-constitutional measures—calls for tax refusal and a run on the banks; they also prepared for violence by arming the political unions. The fact that the Whig Reform Bill was designed only to enfranchise householders in the towns, and copyholders and leaseholders in the counties, meant that unlike 1819 (when the main demand was universal male suffrage) the interests of the middle-class and working-class reformers were at variance. The former made political capital out of the threat of violence presented by the latter, but hoped timely concessions would avert violence. The concessions were made, and the cause of universal franchise was temporarily lost.

The working-class radicals renewed their demands in the Chartist movement of the late 1830s, and combined assertion of constitutional principles with rhetorical emphasis on the value of preparing for armed rebellion. The tendency to stand on their constitutional rights is illustrated by an incident in Newcastle. When the corporation gave notice that 'tumultuous assemblages' of the Chartists would not be allowed in the borough, the Chartists posted a placard with their reply:

> *Whereas*, Certain men calling themselves the Corporation of Newcastle-on-Tyne, have presumed to call in question the inalienable right of Englishmen to meet, discuss and petition the Queen and Parliament for a redress of their grievances . . . we, the council of the Northern Political Union, proclaim to the people of this Borough and the surrounding neighbourhood, that it is their duty to meet for the exercise of this Constitutional right. . . . A meeting will be held in the Forth every evening at half past six (Thompson (ed.), *The Early Chartists*, 175–6).

The Chartists drew not only on the programme of the earlier reform movement, but on its methods. It was decided to hold a People's Parliament or convention. In order to maintain legality (Corresponding Societies were still illegal) and to increase the impression of mass support, delegates to the convention were selected at large open air meetings. These were often accompanied by great torchlight processions. After the general convention had been held delegates reported back at local meetings. The fears aroused by the less constitutional elements of the Chartist programme were expressed by an anxious magistrate of Penzance on learning that deputies from the convention were to hold a meeting:

> Much fear has been felt by the quiet part of the Community. On the one hand, these delegates recommend the deluded People to buy a musket, telling them how well it looks on the Chimney Piece if kept clean and ready for use—and on the other urging them to resist the Poor Law (ibid., 187).

But the Chartists themselves for the most part stressed that they had a constitutional right to bear arms. An article in the *Northern Liberator* claimed that the constitution 'lays it emphatically down, both as a *right* and a *duty*, for *all* Englishmen to be armed for self-defence, and for the defence of their rights and liberties' (ibid., 135). The convention launched a mass petition to parliament, but had to decide on what subsequent actions to call for. Their suggestions included a run on the banks, converting paper money into gold, boycotting goods which carried customs duty, boycotting shopkeepers who did not support the Chartists, arming and drilling. There was an attempt to call a general strike in 1839, but it ended in failure due to lack of support from the then weak trade unions, confusion and disagreement as to whether the strike would also be a signal for armed rebellion, and arrests of the best known Chartists. In 1842 the Chartists assumed political leadership of a series of strikes in the Midlands and the North, which had started as protests against wage-cuts, and strikers passed resolutions pledging themselves to stay out until the charter was accepted. Again the government arrested Chartist leaders, and the workers were starved into submission.

The demand for universal male suffrage was not totally realized until 1918. And it was not until this date that the vote was extended partially to women, though an interesting element of the early franchise movements was the active role played by women, and the occasional and tentative raising of the demand for votes for women. At Peterloo according to a contemporary pamphlet: 'A number of Female Reformers, amounting to 150 came from Oldham and another from Royton. . . . The Females of Royton bore two Red Flags, one inscribed "Let us die like men and not be sold as slaves", the other "Annual Parliaments and Universal Suffrage" ' (Ramelson, *The Petticoat Rebellion*, 68–9).

In 1905 the quiet constitutional campaign for women's suffrage which had been continuing since the 1860s was transformed by the militancy of the Suffragettes, who took to flamboyant and often unconstitutional action to press home their demands for the central symbol of women's rights, the vote. The methods of the Suffragettes included mass processions and rallies; heckling and sometimes attacking politicians; raids on the House of Commons and chaining themselves to its railings; hunger striking in prison and picketing outside; and—especially in the last two years of militancy—breaking windows, setting fire to letter boxes, and other attacks on private and public property. Mrs Pankhurst defended damage to cricket pavilions, golf greens and bowling greens which had, she said, 'the direct and practical object of reminding the dull and self-satisfied English public that when the liberties of English women were being stolen from them it was no time to think of sport' (Mitchell, *The Fighting Pankhursts*, 33).

When Christabel Pankhurst defended herself in court against the charge of inciting a crowd to rush the House of Commons she quoted Gladstone: 'I am sorry to say that if no instructions had ever been addressed in political crises to the people of this country except to remember to hate violence and to love order, the liberties of this people would never have been attained' (*Unshackled*, 109). The Suffragettes were drawing on the experience of the reform movements of the previous century, in particular prior to 1832. David Thomson generalizes that 'repeatedly throughout the century reforms were effected only as concessions to extreme pressure from below, and as alternatives to riot' (Thomson, *England in the Nineteenth Century*, 40).

Trade unions

Perhaps the most sustained violence has occurred not in movements for the vote but in labour struggles, though in Britain these struggles have been frequently conducted with great restraint. The development of the trade union movement provides a particularly interesting study in the use of direct action. Early trade union organization was often designed to obey the letter of the law whilst in practice flouting the ban on the combination of workmen by forming 'friendly societies' for mutual insurance. Early trade union activity was in part an attempt to claim constitutional rights of free speech, assembly and association on behalf of labour, and in part an assertion of new rights—the right to strike and the associated right of peaceful picketing. The nature of trade union organization and the method of the strike also illustrate how extra-parliamentary organization and methods can either be incorporated into parliamentary democracy, or can provide the power base and pattern for future revolution as envisaged by the syndicalists.

The early trade union movement involved at certain periods physical attacks on property. The attempts by artisans to prevent, under the onset of industrialization, the disintegration of the old guild system which preserved their rights led to the government banning combination in the early eighteenth century, and to their making the breaking of machinery into a capital offence early in the nineteenth. The best known outbreak of machine breaking came at the beginning of the nineteenth century when a highly organized movement among framework-knitters systematically destroyed new frames which reduced the need for labour. Luddism spread from the Midlands, where the frames were kept in the workers' cottages, to the manufacturing districts of Lancashire and Yorkshire, where it was necessary to make planned raids on the machinery in the factories. Machine breaking was also accompanied by a number of riots in the manufacturing towns.

But the degree of violence was normally limited. Edward Thompson discusses the 'direct action' resorted to by trade unionists when unionism was illegal—boycotting blackleg workers, sabotaging their machinery or throwing bricks through the windows of unpopular masters. At times this action took the form of physical assault, and occasionally more drastic attempts to blow up workshops or kill individuals. But commonly: 'such direct action was carefully controlled within limits imposed by the moral culture of the working community. . . . Luddism was an extension of this kind of direct action, but it also was carefully controlled within the same unspoken code' (Thompson, *The Making of the English Working Class*, 515). The Luddites also claimed that in breaking the new machines they were simply enforcing their constitutional and legal rights. 'The framework-knitters felt that every statute which might have afforded them protection was abrogated or ignored, while every attempt to enforce their "rights" by trade union action was illegal' (ibid., 533). They appealed to their rights under the charter granted by Charles II, which gave deputies appointed by the Framework-Knitters' Company the power to destroy badly made goods.

Nearly twenty years later agricultural labourers in the south of England, rebelling against increasing poverty and unemployment and the use of the Poor Law to put gangs of paupers to work, began to break up threshing-machines, and to burn ricks of unpopular farmers. G. D. H. Cole comments that apart from the occasional ducking of overseers 'there was a complete absence of violence to persons; in the entire revolt the labourers appear not to have killed or wounded a single person' (*A Short History of the British Working Class Movement*, vol. 1, 110). The Hammonds note in their study of *The Village Labourer* that the destruction of machinery 'was not merely an instinct of violence, there was method and reason in it. Threshing was one of the few kinds of work left that provided the labourer with a means of existence above starvation level' (220-1).

The 1830 movement was crushed and many men who took part in it were transported. It was not until the 1870s that there was a brief revival of militancy resulting in a series of strikes for shorter hours and higher wages. After initial concessions the landed gentry and farmers tried to crush the strikers and tried 'lock-outs'. Agricultural depression and a reduced demand for labour owing to increasing use of land for pasture destroyed the labourers' trade union movement.

In the same period industrial workers were gaining new recognition and rights. The 1871 Trade Union Bill gave trade unions legal status. But this measure was coupled with a Bill providing for strict penalties against 'intimidation', obstruction and picketing and for breach of contract. However, in 1875 trade union agitation led to repeal of the provision for imprisonment for breach of contract, and peaceful picketing was made legal.

The period following this successful claim to the legal right to organize industrial action saw the development of unionism among the unskilled workers, for example: in the Dock Strike of 1889; the assertion of the right to strike by workers subjected to quasi-military discipline, like the railway workers who finally won this right in 1911; and the use of strikes to enforce unionism among workers in the industry—a policy of pit stoppages was successfully adopted by the South Wales Miners' Federation in 1906.* In the early years of this century strikes were called on a nationwide as well as a purely local or regional scale, and in the years just before the First World War the idea of the sympathetic strike was gaining support. Cole comments:

> The sympathetic strike had been a powerful factor in the success of the strikes of 1911, and thereafter it was preached by the adherents of the 'New Unionism' as a weapon to be freely used in industrial conflicts. The railwaymen were constantly receiving requests from workers on strike to refuse to carry 'tainted' goods (*A Short History of the British Working Class Movement*, vol. III, 92).

The concept of the sympathetic strike lay behind the 'general strike' of 1926, when the Trades Union Congress called for a general strike in support of the claims by the miners.

The idea of a general strike had been part of the theory of the labour movement for a century. In 1832 Benbow had advocated a 'Grand National Holiday' to last one month, which would halt both the economy and the administration, and enable the strikers to take over. Tom Mann had much more recently put forward the syndicalist theory of the general strike which would usher in the social revolution. But when it came the trade union leaders stressed throughout that the general strike was limited to economic aims and strictly constitutional. The government, on the other hand, maintained it was a challenge to constitutionalism. Not only did Churchill in the *British Gazette* see it as the signal for red revolution, but even Baldwin said that the strike would bring the country nearer to civil war than it had been for centuries. There was, however, relatively little violence against persons, though there was some fighting in parts of London between strikers and the 'specials' brought in to reinforce the police. More surprisingly there was very little systematic sabotage even though this would have reduced the possibility of strike-breaking. Julian Symons notes in his study of the 1926 General Strike that the most important attempt at sabotage was the 'derailment of the volunteer-manned Flying Scotsman at Cramlington near Newcastle, on the seventh day of the strike' (*The General Strike*, 104). The most radical

---

* The miners in South Wales were responsive to syndicalist ideas and the South Wales' Miners' Reform Movement advocated reliance on 'direct action' to achieve workers' control in the mines. These proposals were made in the 1912 pamphlet: *The Miners' Next Step*, which was published by the Unofficial Reform Committee of the South Wales Miners' Federation.

aspect of the strike was not the few violent incidents but the tendency for the strikers to take things increasingly into their own hands without waiting for orders from the central leadership.

The constitutionalism of industrial action has been an issue not only in relation to the general strike, but in relation to its possible use for political goals. This issue was most debated within the Labour movement in 1919. The miners had voted in February by an overwhelming majority for a strike to ensure the nationalization of the mines, and with other sections of the trade union movement had called for action to force the government to lift the blockade against Germany, end conscription and release conscientious objectors. The Executive's report to the Labour Party Conference in June stated: 'Many resolutions have been received at the Head Office, indicating that there are some sections of the Movement anxious that an organized attempt to defeat the Government's political policy by direct industrial action should be discussed by a joint Conference representative of both the political and industrial movements' (Miliband, *Parliamentary Socialism*, 68). At the conference the chairman of the party argued that use of the strike for political purposes would be welcomed by 'few responsible leaders'.

> We are either constitutionalists or we are not constitutionalists.
> If we are constitutionalists, if we believe in the efficacy of the
> political weapon (and we do, or why do we have a Labour Party?)
> then it is both unwise and undemocratic because we fail to get a
> majority at the polls to turn round and demand that we should
> substitute industrial action (ibid., 69).

But although the Labour leaders ignored demands by miners and other unionists that action should be taken to ensure withdrawal of British troops in Russia, the threat of British involvement in the Polish attack against Russia in 1920 inspired both unofficial and then official commitment to trade union resistance. Dockers in London refused to handle ammunition and other supplies which *The Jolly George* was due to carry to Poland. The railwaymen's executive also urged its members to black supplies to Poland. When a few weeks later the Soviet army repulsed the Polish attack and began advancing into Poland, the British government threatened to support the Poles. The Labour movement created a Council of Action, and local councils sprang up throughout the country. The Labour Party Executive Committee and Trades Union Congress Parliamentary Committee warned the government that 'the whole industrial power of the organized workers will be used to defeat this war'. A National Labour Conference was called which endorsed the call for a general strike to prevent British troops being sent to Poland, but Lloyd George had already promised Labour leaders that the most the government would do would be to supply arms.

Anti-war movement

The general strike was intended prior to 1914 to be the weapon used by the labour movement to prevent war between the European states. The general strike failed to materialize, but there was in Britain a widespread movement against the war. During war time it is normal to suspend certain constitutional liberties enjoyed in time of peace, and public speeches, newspaper articles or the distribution of leaflets may be regarded as acts of sedition. A number of protesters in Britain, including Bertrand Russell, were charged and imprisoned for these activities between 1914–18. On the other hand, during the war a new constitutional right, that of conscientious objection, was also being established, though this right was not fully recognized until the Second World War. Between 1916–18 about 6,000 objectors were arrested, court-martialled and in due course sentenced to jail. When their sentence was over the process began again. Approximately 600 men were sent to prison twice, and 500 three times. The army also indulged in more direct forms of intimidation—34 men were shipped to France and sentenced to death publicly, this sentence then being commuted to ten years' imprisonment. As a result of their treatment in jail 71 men died; many others suffered from tuberculosis.

The most dangerous form of action during war time from the point of view of the authorities is the mass opposition entailed in mutiny. Even if a mutiny is only a form of trade union protest against working conditions, as was the case in the mutinies of Spithead and the Nore during the Napoleonic Wars, it poses a threat to the entire war effort. During 1917 a wave of mutinies spread through the French army based on widespread weariness with the war itself, but sparked off by the mass slaughter resulting from General Nivelle's offensive at the end of April. The mutinies started in the Sixth Army which had suffered worst in the Nivelle offensive. Troops ordered to return to the front refused to go and laid down their arms and spread disaffection to other troops passing through. Rumours spread. Norman Cantor notes in his account:

> There were stories of how in another army in another part of France a regiment had seized an entire town. . . . Another battalion had marched itself off to the safety of an adjacent forest. Still another had captured a train and set out for Paris (*The Age of Protest*, 55).

But although the mutinies continued until September most of the mutineers allowed themselves to be driven back to the trenches, or went of their own accord. They did not turn their arms against the government or even their own officers. Cantor comments: 'Officers were not so much defied as ignored. In this respect the typical mutiny resembled a work stoppage more than revolution' (ibid., 57). The mutinies were manifestations of the same kind of unorganized rebellion as the desertion rate—by 1917 estimated at 30,000 a year. Many mutineers were shot, often without benefit of court martial, so that the total of executions is unknown. The mutineers won only a tacit victory—the French general staff did not try to make their demoralized armies advance again until the autumn of 1918.

Direct action and constitutional rights today

This brief sketch of some previous movements indicates the difficulty of drawing clear distinctions between constitutional and direct action in situations where constitutional rights had not been fully established, or where under threat of war or internal revolt the government has rescinded these rights. But it does suggest that Rocker is correct in arguing that defiance of the law and popular pressure are part of the process of establishing such rights as free speech, a free press and free association. It also suggests that movements using direct action may succeed in establishing new rights once not considered either constitutional or legal, such as the right to strike, or the right to conscientious objection. Indeed, over long periods certain forms of activity may be tacitly accepted as semi-legitimate even though the force of law can be used to prevent them. Currently sit-ins seem to be becoming an established mode of militant but peaceful protest. Squatting in empty houses has also attained to a similar status of half-acceptance by the authorities combined with periodic attempts to clamp down on it.

A glance back into the past also indicates that even rights which have been legally won may be endangered again—particularly in times of crisis. The freedom of speech, of public assembly, and of procession may require constant reassertion—and at times this assertion may be held to be illegal. But the rights most constantly liable to attack are those of trade unionists. Whilst from the standpoint of trade unionists strikes are necessary guarantees of their bargaining power in wage claims and in the protection of workers' rights, from the standpoint of both employers and government industrial disputes are wasteful and damaging.

So whilst Labour Party and trade union leaders have almost always shrunk from using direct action in order to promote a political confrontation, they have not always been able to avoid the dilemma posed by governmental and court restrictions on trade union rights within the purely industrial field. The unions have not been able to take for granted their legal immunity. The apparent legal guarantees of 1875 were jeopardized by the Taff Vale decision by the House of Lords in 1901 that the Taff Vale Company had a right to receive damages from the railwaymen's union for the damage done to the company's business during the strike and the attempts to stop blackleg labour. The threat posed to union funds, and their right to organize industrial action, was removed again by legislation in 1906. After the 1926 general strike, the government brought in comprehensive legislation to curb the power of trade unions by outlawing both the general strike and most sympathetic strikes, restricting the right to picket and enabling the government to issue legal injunctions against 'illegal' strikes. The 1927 Act was not repealed until the return of a Labour government in 1945.

The potentiality of trade unions for disrupting trade, specific services, and the economy in general have meant, however, that governments are continually inclined to consider curbing union powers. Tentative steps in this direction made by the Labour government in the mid-1960s have been followed by the Conservative government's Industrial Relations Act of 1971.

This Act encouraged trade unions to be registered with a registrar who would have power to oversee their rules. Unions which did not register, and persons taking industrial action without the authority of registered unions, were made legally liable to pay compensation for a wide range of 'unfair industrial practices'. Even registered unions could be similarly penalized for many 'unfair' practices, for example, in relation to closed shop disputes or if they embarked on forms of 'sympathetic' industrial action, though they could generally escape liability for the most common 'unfair' practice, namely inducing breaches of contract.

The Industrial Relations legislation faced the trade union movement with the decision whether to take industrial action to resist the Bill before it became law, and whether to defy the law and undertake civil disobedience after the Act had been passed. Militants did call a widely supported one-day stoppage to protest against the Bill. The Trades Union Congress officially endorsed a policy of non-co-operation, requiring affiliated unions not to register as required under the Act, and not to co-operate with the Industrial Relations Court. The latter policy was partially dropped almost immediately following a court decision relating to a dockers' dispute over use of container lorries which were taking work away from the docks. Affiliated unions were now permitted by the TUC to use the court to the extent necessary to defend themselves against legal action by others.

In the case of the dockers the court's decisions did precipitate a confrontation between the state and the unions. Shop stewards who were trying to 'black' container lorries, and picketing outside a container firm, were ordered to desist, and when they defied the order were threatened with imprisonment for contempt of court. The first time the shop stewards were sentenced to imprisonment by the court for blacking lorries a hurried appeal against this decision led to its reversal, and a national dock strike planned in protest was averted. Shortly afterwards, stewards organizing the picketing of a container firm were sent to prison for contempt. Not only dockers, but many printers, miners and engineers walked out in protest. Industrial action began to spread and the TUC officially endorsed a call for a one-day general strike. Thousands of trade unionists picketed the prison. After the unusually short time of five days, the court decided that the jailed dockers should be released. The TUC called off the general strike, but a national dock strike in protest against the effects of containerization went ahead.

However, at the same time as the unions demonstrated their power by securing the release of the dockers, they also suffered a serious setback. When the dockers' union, the Transport and General Workers Union, was originally brought before the Industrial Relations Court because some of its stewards were blacking container lorries, the court made the union responsible for disciplining its own shop stewards. The union was fined for its contempt of court in failing to obey the court's order to take reasonable steps to stop the blacking, and the court further held that continued failure to take such steps could render all the union's assets liable to seizure. The industrial court's decision was reversed on appeal, but the Law Lords upheld the original decision, which left trade unions in the kind of uncertainty that prevailed after the 1901 Taff Vale Judgment. It was, in fact, the decision of the House of Lords which enabled the Industrial Relations Court to release the jailed dockers, on the ground that it was now the union's job to discipline them.

Another government measure which promoted thoughts of defiance among law-abiding members of the community, and evoked echoes of the past Labour movement, was the 1971 Housing Finance ('Fair Rents') Bill designed to raise council house rents. A number of Labour-controlled councils declared their intention of refusing to implement the Bill when it became law. The London Borough of Camden was the first to announce an official decision not to co-operate with the Act, the week after it received Royal Assent at the end of July 1972. The councillors faced the possibility of being charged personally for the resulting loss of rent and of eventual imprisonment for non-payment. Where councils decided to implement the Act some militant tenants associations planned rent strikes in protest.

While many Labour controlled councils initially voted to defy the Act, the numbers dwindled under financial pressure. Camden agreed to implement the Act in mid-January 1973, because the government was withholding subsidies for local services. Early in March Merthyr Tydfil council ended five months of non-co-operation 'in the long term interests of the council house tenants'. Eleven rebel councillors in the ex-mining town of Clay Cross, Derbyshire, had been personally surcharged £7000 by early March.

Disobedient councils could cite as a precedent the actions of Labour councillors in the 1920s who raised the amount of relief under the Poor Law without government authorization. The boards administering the

Poor Law in the most distressed areas were faced with paying out enormous sums. In 1921 the Poplar Borough Council refused to pay the London County Council for locally run LCC services as a protest against lack of funds for relief in the poorest areas. The Poplar councillors were sent to prison for contempt of court—but the government made the Metropolitan Common Poor Fund more responsible for poor relief as a result of the Poplar protest. However, local councils who tried to raise the rate of poor relief above the scale fixed by the government ran into trouble with the Ministry of Health. The Poor Law Guardians at West Ham and Chester-le-Street were replaced in 1926 by commissioners appointed direct by the Ministry.

During 1972 there occurred a quite different example of non-co-operation intended to support local interests against the central government, when a number of Welsh magistrates refused to fine Welsh language campaigners who had withheld payment of their TV licences to emphasize their demand for an all-Welsh TV and radio channel. Judicial support for protesters brought before the courts for disobedience—fairly common among eighteenth-century juries and even judges—has been rare in contemporary movements in Britain. The magistrates' gesture was an indication of the extent of support for the Welsh language campaign, which resulted in nearly one hundred people being sent to jail in 1971 for painting out road signs, attacking TV plants, and interrupting court proceedings.

The continuities in protest are based partly on conscious borrowing from a tradition of dissent, but often stem from a spontaneous reaction to circumstances. The recent factory sit-ins, for example, arouse associations with the American sit-in strikes of the 1930s, but were not directly inspired by them. However once a campaign has begun the participants may look back to the past to seek for parallels.

The history of the movements for radical reform provides many precedents for various forms of non-co-operation and direct action being revived in the present—whether by defiant magistrates and Labour councillors, by tenants staging rent strikes, or by demonstrators chaining themselves to railings. The fact that these forms of protest were undertaken by movements which have, in the eyes of many, now attained to historical respectability and political legitimacy constitutes a kind of justification for direct action in the present: the justification from appeal to precedent.

Relevance of the past

But apart from appealing to historical sentiment and tradition, reference to the struggles of the past is valid as a means of putting current unrests into perspective, because modern disturbances tend to be viewed by many in the context of an idealized and mythical picture of constitutional progress. The brief references to past struggles in this chapter illustrate the fact that, even after Britain had achieved constitutional government, liberal and democratic reforms were won often by disobedience and the threat of rebellion. Most European countries experienced much greater popular violence during the same period. The French Revolution occurred whilst British suffrage societies were promoting peaceful agitation for the vote. In 1848 Britain was one of the few countries where a popular uprising against the government did not occur.

The relatively peaceful nature of political agitation in Britain was due partly to the relatively liberal nature of its government. But if the history of popular movements in the United States is compared with that of Britain, it is clear that despite the democratic spirit of American politics the efforts of impoverished farmers, of industrial workers and of immigrant groups to establish basic social and economic rights have involved more prolonged disobedience and greater violence. The history of American dissent is relevant to current debates about 'law and order' in the United States. Richard Rubenstein comments:

> Whether in the White House, Congress or the street, reactions to recent riots and demonstrations reveal a widely held belief that such episodes are 'un-American'—rare occurrences in American life . . . this is a false assumption. For more than two hundred years, from the Indian wars and farmer uprisings of the eighteenth century to the labor-management and racial disturbances of the twentieth, the United States had experienced regular episodes of serious mass violence related to the social, political and economic objectives of insurgent groups (*Rebels in Eden*, 7).

Rubenstein cites as an example the revolts of debtor farmers between the 1740s and 1790s in the Wars of the Regulators, the War of the New Hampshire Grants, the Shays Rebellion and the Whiskey Rebellion:

> In state after state, hated laws provoked first civil disobedience, then physical attacks on tax collectors and other law enforcers, and finally the closing down of courts to prevent issuance of mortgage foreclosures and indictments . . . the rebels established *de facto* control over the western counties of several states, lasting in some cases for several years (ibid., 25–6).

The general thesis put forward by Rubenstein was accepted in a report to the National Commission on Causes and Prevention of Violence submitted by the Task Force on Violent Aspects of Protest and Confrontation. This Report sums up that: 'there has been relatively little violence accompanying contemporary demonstration and group protest'. It also concludes:

> Our research finds that mass protest is an essentially political
> phenomenon engaged in by normal people; that demonstrations are
> increasingly being employed by a variety of groups, ranging from
> students and blacks to middle-class professionals, public employees,
> and policemen; that violence when it occurs, is usually not planned,
> but arises out of an interaction between protesters and responding
> authorities; that violence has frequently accompanied the efforts of
> deprived groups to achieve status in American society (in Skolnick
> (ed.), *The Politics of Protest*, xix).

The conclusion that protest now, as in the past, is in the main a response
by ordinary citizens to a sense of injustice, and that compared with the
past current protests are less prone to take violent forms also holds good
for Britain; though both in the past and the present levels of violence have
generally been lower in this country. The history of both the United
States and Britain also suggests that the most serious forms of violence
have not been attacks on the government, but attacks on other groups in
the community. The Gordon Riots of 1780 aimed against the Catholics
in London were more vicious than the demonstrations in favour of
Wilkes—though some of the same people took part. Irishmen participating
in the 1863 New York Draft Riot attacked not only draft offices, but the
negroes whom they saw as strike breakers.

The history of the movement in Britain towards universal suffrage also
reveals the two-edged nature of violence. On the one hand, the threat of
serious rioting or armed insurrection was a major spur to the government
to make concessions, especially when the army and police forces at the
disposal of the authorities could not easily suppress major outbreaks of
violence. On the other hand, violent incidents could often be used as a
means of dividing the movement and as a pretext for repression, as the role
of government agents in instigating plots to promote violence clearly
illustrates. Third, it appears that, especially in the early movement for
parliamentary reform associated with Wilkes, mass demonstrations which
were primarily peaceful could verge into mob rioting through pressure of
numbers, tactless provocation by the authorities and the volatility of the
crowd. Frequently demonstrations were good humoured, but the potentiality to riot was an essential part of the campaign for constitutional
liberties and parliamentary reform, given the nature of the popular
movement at that time. This fact would not have been surprising to
eighteenth-century constitutionalists steeped in the Roman classics and
the role of the plebians in the Roman republic. As Machiavelli observed in
his discussion of Roman politics:

> And if it be said that these are strange means, to hear constantly the
> cries of the people furious against the Senate . . . to see the
> populace rush tumultously through the streets, close their houses,

and even leave the city of Rome,—I reply . . . that every free state ought to afford the people the opportunity of giving vent, so to say, to their ambition . . . when the people wanted to obtain a law they resorted to some of the extremes of which we have just spoken, or they refused to enroll themselves to serve in the wars, so that the Senate was obliged to satisfy them in some measure. The demands of a free people are rarely pernicious to their liberty (*The Prince and the Discourses*, 120).

3 The politics of direct action campaigns

Examples of direct action cannot be understood in isolation from the campaigns in which they occur. It is necessary to consider the possible repercussions of direct action in order to judge its effectiveness and its drawbacks, and therefore to make wider judgments about its legitimacy.

It is not easy to compare direct action campaigns taking place at different times and in differing circumstances—but it is possible to see certain common elements in the planning of direct action strategy, and common tendencies among movements resorting to disruption and disobedience. The obvious differences between movements are due to the kind of people taking part, their political beliefs and goals, the response of the authorities, and the impact of internal or international events.

Many of the strategic aspects of direct action can be illustrated from the Suffragette movement in Britain. Although the Suffragettes' concept of 'militancy' excluded many of the ideological overtones of direct action today, it provides a basic model of unconstitutional action, and in discussing it we have the advantage of historical hindsight.

Contemporary movements against apartheid, nuclear weapons and racial discrimination provide a wider range of evidence about the tactical strengths and the political limits of direct action. This chapter examines the Stop The Seventies Tour campaign, direct action in the CND movement, and the evolution of the American civil rights struggle, and tries to suggest some conditions promoting success or failure, and some reasons why direct action movements turn either to a broader political strategy or towards violence.

The Suffragettes

The Suffragettes started from the premise that constitutional methods alone would not achieve votes for women. They could appeal to the lessons of history to show that previous struggles for the vote had not been entirely peaceable. When Christabel Pankhurst asked Lloyd George in court 'whether any interference with public order took place in connection with previous movements for franchise reform?', she received the answer that it did.

The Suffragettes also claimed with particular relevance that in the cause of women's suffrage, constitutional methods had been tried and failed. A conciliation committee of MPs, set up in 1910 to try to resolve different views on the question of giving women the vote, commented:

This question is as urgent as it is important. It is forty years since the first Suffrage Bill passed its second reading in the House of Commons. The patience and ability of the women of the older Suffrage societies deserved an earlier reward. The failure of Parliaments to give effect to an opinion which they have repeatedly avowed, would, if continued, justify women in complaining that in regard to them the Constitution had broken down (Pankhurst, *Unshackled*, 152).

The committee went on to give implicit support to the Suffragette case for militancy by adding that 'the painful struggle of the past four years is an experience which no one would wish to see repeated'. The Pankhursts themselves came to espouse militancy after their experience of the work put into campaigning for the 1905 Woman Suffrage Bill, which lacking government support was talked out by its opponents.

The first advantage of unorthodox methods is that they are more dramatic than most constitutional activities, and therefore tend to rouse attention. Christabel Pankhurst comments:

Suffrage meetings, however large, were affairs of words, and the words of voteless women were not 'news'. But militancy was news, was current history. . . . The Press became our best ally. That super-journalist, W T Stead, said to Mother: 'People always swear at you before they swear by you' (ibid., 56).

Publicity is the first stage in putting pressure on the government to take action. Christabel Pankhurst records that when she led a deputation to see Balfour, and he was asked why his government had not given the vote to women, he replied: 'Well, to tell you the truth, your cause is not in the swim' (ibid., 58).

Direct action involves not only creating a stir, but posing a more or less direct challenge to the authorities, and forcing them either to lose face or to pay the movement the compliment of taking repressive action against it. The Suffragette tactic of systematically interrupting public meetings held by the Liberals frequently succeeded in making their opponents look ridiculous. When the Liberals resorted to excluding all women from their meetings, the Suffragettes responded by smuggling themselves into meeting halls well in advance, thus promoting further police measures to try to protect ministers from their attentions. The *Yorkshire Telegraph* commented when Asquith came to Sheffield: 'It is not a very dignified proceeding, to have to smuggle a Prime Minister into the city, yet that was the sort of triumphal entry Mr Asquith made' (ibid., 127).

When, however, the government took legal action against the Suffragettes this move greatly assisted their cause. In October 1906, ten women were arrested after trying to address a crowd outside the Houses of

Parliament, and sentenced to a £10 fine or two months in prison. Inside prison the women were allocated to 'Second Division' treatment, like common criminals. Theresa Billington's recollections of the militant suffrage movement note that: 'The first phase of the movement came suddenly to an end, and we who had struggled and foundered in shifting sand found ourselves on firm ground' (in Fulford, *Votes for Women*, 151). Roger Fulford, in his study, judges that at this point the newspapers which had 'formerly treated the [women's Social and Political] Union members as a lark', now took them seriously. The government saw its mistake, released two women on health grounds and transferred the others to 'First Division' treatment. But the mistake had been made.

The effectiveness of confrontation with the authorities depends on the success of the movement in mobilizing its own supporters to greater efforts, in winning the active sympathy of those who already agree with their aims, and in gaining new supporters among the general public and those with political influence—for example, the press and the elected representatives. Theresa Billington explains how in 1906 the Home Secretary 'supplied to the movement the needed stimulus of passionate enthusiasm, the spirit that always rises under oppression'. Roger Fulford estimates that the prison sentences brought about 'the dangerous conjunction of the militants with the constitutional suffragists . . . disapproval was swallowed up in indignation at the severity of the Government and admiration for its victims' (*Votes for Women*, 151).

The impact on a wider public depends partly on the shift in perception created by militant tactics—the demonstration of the strength of determination and refusal to stay passive. Moreover, by posing a direct challenge to the government, the Suffragettes altered political perception of their cause and indicated a new impatience, and a new willingness to struggle as well as petition for their right to vote.

Third, by harassing ministers, trying to march on the House of Commons and going to jail (and later by going on hunger strike) the Suffragettes dramatized the reality of their sense of injustice—and by their actions tended to polarize attitudes on what had become a central political question. A Liberal wrote in 1907 that due to Mrs Pankhurst 'an academic issue for half a century, became actual and vital, as it were in a night . . . whatever we may think of her methods, we cannot doubt that they have shaken the walls of Westminster' (Pankhurst, *Unshackled*, 60).

Apart from enhancing public awareness of the injustice suffered and the political significance of their cause, the Suffragettes relied mainly on exciting admiration and sympathy, even among those who disagreed with their aims, or their tactics. Roger Fulford comments that when in 1908 the Suffragettes appealed at a meeting in Trafalgar Square for public help to rush the House of Commons, and three leading members were sentenced to several months in prison, their punishment 'commanded the respect and sympathy of the newspapers. . . . There was also a steady stream of protest about the treatment of the three ladies—especially the point about First or Second Division treatment—in the House of Commons' (*Votes for Women*, 191). Millicent Garrett Fawcett, a leading Suffragist opposed to militant methods, wrote: 'What those endured who underwent the hunger strike and the anguish of forcible feeding can hardly be overestimated. Their courage made a very deep impression on the public and touched the imagination of the whole country' (*Women's Suffrage*, 66).

But a campaign aiming to alter government policy normally has to move beyond the stage of dramatizing the issue, mildly embarrassing the authorities, and mobilizing a degree of general sympathy—unless influential political bodies in and outside the government are prepared to support the cause at this point. If influential support is not forthcoming the choice lies between building up a longer-term political alliance, moving into a phase of mass resistance to government policy, or escalating the threat of disruption and disorder inherent in direct action to a politically critical level.

The Suffragettes could not, of course, rely on the immediate voting strength of women to try to buy political concessions from either the government or the opposition. They did have the political potential to be gained from future voting power which might be available to a party which granted women the vote—but it was questionable how far women voters as a whole could be expected to react with appropriate gratitude. Mrs Pankhurst and her eldest daughter also decided against linking their cause with the new Labour Party. Though the Party supported votes for women in principle, they feared that in practice it would not be prepared to give this policy priority. They saw the Women's Liberal Federation acting as a vote getting appendage of the Liberal Party which always had other priorities than women's suffrage. Christabel Pankhurst writes: 'Already there were some Labourists saying that other things must be dealt with before women got the vote' (*Unshackled*, 69–70). They also feared they would split the movement by attaching themselves to one political party, and preferred to unite women as an independent force. Therefore, although the Suffragettes did engage in vigorous election campaigning, they did so largely as an extension of their tactic of harrying the Liberals, from 1906 the dominant party, and by trying to lose the Liberal candidate votes.

The Suffragettes never approached the stage of being able to undermine the government by the strength of their resistance, although sustained activities by the Suffragettes and the operations of the Cat and Mouse Act may have induced a sense of weariness and distaste amongst some of those who had to deal with the militants. Christabel Pankhurst voices the opinion that in 1914:

Judges and magistrates were getting very tired of trying and
sentencing Suffragettes. They hated the whole thing. They had
endeavoured to persuade and compel the women to give in and they
had failed. Their only remaining hope was that the Government
would give in. The judges and magistrates were becoming more and
more a force on our side (ibid., 270–1).

Since, however, the Suffragettes were becoming increasingly isolated
from some of their former colleagues, and by the summer of 1914 the
constitutional suffragists were arguably of greater political significance,
and able to command greater numbers as well as influential support, her
judgment is questionable.

Neither in fact was the Suffragette strategy ever geared to the concept of
promoting mass resistance and non-co-operation. After the break between
the Pankhursts and some of their initial supporters in 1907, it was the
latter who, through the Women's Freedom League, promoted tactics of
non-co-operation and civil disobedience, for example, the principle of
'no taxation without representation', and a boycott of the 1911 Census.
In 1912 the Pethick-Lawrences left the Union over the issue of whether
the Suffragettes should turn from 'mild' or 'symbolic' militancy to
attacks on property. At this stage the Pankhurst strategy became one of
sabotage and smashing windows. The Pankhursts' model had from the
beginning been the threat of violent disruption and disorder as the lever to
gain concessions from the government. Christabel recalls that they had
drawn this lesson from government reactions to a protest by the unemployed in Manchester in 1905. Following this protest, transformed by the
press into a riot, the government, which had been delaying the Unemployment Bill, saw that it was expeditiously passed by parliament. Between
1906 and 1914 the failure of parliament to pass legislation giving women
the vote resulted in the development of the Suffragette strategy from the
heckling of Liberal ministers to the support of arson.

This brief outline of the initial gains from militancy and the final
drawbacks suggests some of the pitfalls inherent in resort to dramatic and
unconventional tactics. The reliance on press publicity, for example,
meant to some extent staging 'stunts' for the papers. There is also a
temptation for any protest group to assume publicity is an indication of
the political impact of their movement. Christabel Pankhurst records
their elation, and that of some long standing Suffragists, when Votes for
Women became 'news'. When Christabel and Annie Kenney went to
prison for the first time in 1905, after interrupting a Liberal meeting,
a veteran Suffragist wrote to the Pankhursts with glee: 'Look at the
newspapers!' (ibid., 56). Before militancy began, the editor of the *Manchester Guardian* told a delegation seeking publicity for women's
suffrage that it was the 'settled policy' of his paper to 'ignore the

question' (Pankhurst, *The Suffragette Movement*, 514).

But if Fulford is correct in his assessment, the early publicity attracted to the efforts of the Suffragettes had more sensational than political value, and they were not taken seriously. 'They provided, to the perceptive eye of an editor, much the same type of copy as a rag by "varsity chaps" on rugger night in Leicester Square' (*Votes for Women*, 151).

Second, attempts to make the authorities look ridiculous are always liable to rebound, so that to the neutral observer it may often have been the Suffragettes' antics which looked ridiculous—especially so long as they were treated with tolerance. Third, there is the inherent drawback that in a constitutional state, the resort to illegal or unconventional protest may split rather than unite those who support the protesters' aim. The Suffragists began by disapproving of Suffragette tactics, and though later they sometimes joined together in demonstrations of solidarity the two movements continued to disagree about methods. Millicent Garrett Fawcett noted the problems created by the Suffragettes for the National Union of Women's Suffrage Societies: 'A few of our own members attacked us because we were not militant; others resigned because they disapproved of the militantism which we had repudiated' (*Women's Suffrage*, 62). By 1909 Fulford calculates that increasing disorders 'had antagonised opinion', and as a result muted public indignation about forcible feeding. He quotes Churchill's comment to a deputation from the League: 'I am bound to say I think your cause has marched backwards' (*Votes for Women*, 211).

These particular drawbacks are not necessarily very important. As noted earlier, even the rather mild martyrdom of brief prison sentences resulted in the Suffragettes being taken seriously, and gaining support from the more constitutionally minded Suffragists. Mrs Fawcett remarks that the tense situation created by disputes about method was 'somewhat relieved by the brutal severity with which some of the militant suffragists were treated. It gave suffragists of all parties another subject on which they were in agreement' (*Women's Suffrage*, 63). Despite Fulford's judgment that the actions of 1909 had lost public sympathy, he also concludes that:

> The seriousness with which Parliament treated the issue of
> woman's suffrage in 1910 must in justice be counted as one of the
> achievements of militancy. For would peaceful parades, lobbying
> Members of Parliament and gatherings in Belgravian drawing-rooms
> have achieved the same end? The debate (though disappointing to
> the ardent spirits of Clement's Inn) was in reality a measure of
> their success (*Votes for Women*, 228).

It is, however, arguable that a more serious defect of unconstitutional methods is the inherent tendency to move towards ever-increasing militancy, a tendency manifesting itself by 1909, but which had brought about much more damaging results by 1914. It is also doubtful how far a movement can rely upon suppression by the authorities to promote solidarity and sympathy.

The very reasons for adopting unconstitutional tactics in the first place may be conducive to increasing militancy and eventually resort to violence. The main argument for not relying on constitutional means—their ineffectiveness—may be adduced after a while for abandoning direct action and turning to sabotage or forms of guerrilla warfare. Moreover, the fact of having taken the step beyond constitutionalism into direct action makes it easier to move a stage further to deliberate violence. Christabel Pankhurst estimated in 1910 that, after five years of Suffragette activity 'mild militancy was more or less played out'. Tactics become monotonous by repetition and cease to impress.

The role of the press is also calculated to encourage demonstrators to provide new forms of drama. Since novelty is news, after a time the same forms of action are likely to become less newsworthy. The element most likely to attract wide coverage is violence, which is assumed to be more or less continuously dramatic. Fulford comments on the dilemma intrinsic to the Suffragettes' strategy:

> Although the publicity was immense, and although even the most
> stubborn foes applauded the ingenuity and eloquence of mother
> and daughter . . . they were committed to a course which was fatal.
> For each of their escapades—disturbances at meetings, intervention
> at by-elections, marches to Westminster in defiance of the police and
> now the use of courts of justice for propaganda—achieved publicity
> but exhausted it. They could only advance by means of fresh
> clashes with law and order. And what would be the consequences of
> these on public opinion? (ibid., 192).

Government policy which involves forcible attempts to suppress unconstitutional action may also foster militancy. Christabel Pankhurst reverts to this point several times:

> Another reason why mild militancy could not avail much longer
> was that our women were beginning to revolt against the one-sided
> violence which they experienced in the course of their attempts to
> persuade the King's Prime Minister. It was being said among them
> that they would prefer to break a window than be themselves thrown
> about and hurt. . . . They were questioning whether . . . they had
> any right to risk personal injury, if a little damage to panes of glass
> would have the same, and indeed more, effect (*Unshackled*, 153–4).

The mood of impatience within a movement which leads protesters to question why they should lay themselves open to injury and arrest, may also lead some of them to the conclusion that the government respects violence more than peaceful protest. The authorities may themselves stimulate this reaction. The Suffragettes took the government at their word when a member of the cabinet said that women did not seriously want the vote because they had not, as men demanding the franchise had done, burned down a castle. A girl who tried to break into a government minister's house to set it on fire wrote a note saying: 'When Cabinet Ministers tell us that violence is the only argument they understand, it becomes our duty to give them that argument' (ibid., 230–1).

The Suffragettes were also very aware of the fact that confronted with the threat of mutiny and civil war over Ulster, the government was eager to appease the pro-Ulster forces. The king met Edward Carson when, on his ministers' advice, he was refusing to meet Mrs Pankhurst. Christabel noted that by 1914: 'Militancy was rapidly winning its victory in the affair of Ulster' (ibid., 266). This comment shows that the assumption underlying Suffragette tactics was that disruption, and threat of greater violence to come, pays political dividends. It is inherent in this model that initial lack of success will promote a militancy which eventually turns to violence. It was also an inappropriate model to be adopted by a movement without either the high level political allies enjoyed by Ulster, or the ability to wage genuine guerrilla warfare or civil war. The fairly marginal destruction of property the Suffragettes embarked upon in 1912 was guaranteed to shock public opinion and to alienate many supporters, without being more than nuisance value to the government. Sylvia Pankhurst deplored the fact that in July 1912 her sister began to organize 'secret arson'—even though she thought that government treatment of the cause 'largely neutralized any harm that incendiarism would work':

> I regarded this new policy with grief and regret, believing it wholly mistaken and unnecessary, deeply deploring the life of furtive destruction it would impose upon the participators, and the harsh punishment it was preparing for them; for these unknown girls there would be no international telegrams; the mead of public sympathy would be attenuated. The old, defiant, symbolic militancy performed in the sight of all, punished with a severity out of all proportion to its damage, if damage there were, had roused an enormous volume of support (*The Suffragette Movement*, 401).

Apart from the political ineffectiveness probably inherent in the policy, the Suffragettes tended after 1912 to lose sight of political considerations, and to centre their activities round Mrs Pankhurst in the game of cat and mouse played between her and the authorities. Christabel's own account emphasizes in the closing years the central role played by her mother and the devotion of her followers. Fulford comments that sabotage tended to be related to the arrests of Mrs Pankhurst: 'As long as the Pethick-

Lawrences were prominent in the Union, militancy was used as a political weapon. The marches on St Stephen's or the smashings of windows were made to coincide with debates at Westminster: it was forceful but not illogical political intimidation' (*Votes for Women*, 300). But after the Pethick-Lawrences left, this political direction was lost. Only Sylvia linked militancy to the wider social causes of the women of the East End where she had her base. In July 1913 she led a large procession of East End workers to Downing Street. This was in her assessment 'the first large-scale demonstration of real popular turbulence the Suffrage movement had shown' (*The Suffragette Movement*, 488).

Because the Suffragettes pursued a strategy of newsworthy exploits or of pure disruption they were not able to focus increasing militancy into politically relevant channels. Up to 1910 their main activities were in effect a determined exercise of basic constitutional rights—to go to political meetings, to join in election activity, and to petition the House of Commons. When the police tried to forbid these activities the Suffragettes remained in a strong rhetorical position. After an early march on the House of Commons Christabel claimed in court that the government was responsible for any disorder that occurred, 'and that their orders to the police had resulted in violence to a perfectly peaceful deputation' (*Unshackled*, 76). But the increase in militancy towards breaking windows or burning pillar boxes meant a decrease in the relevance of the protest— action was not directed to the issue of voting rights or to specific grievances of women which it was hoped the vote would remedy. This gap between 'militancy' and immediate relevance of the action arose in part out of the nature of the Suffragettes' goal—which did not readily provide local targets for action or the possibility of limited victories.

Stop the Tour campaign

If the Suffragette movement is compared with a more limited contemporary campaign, which also relied primarily on publicity and on the power of disruption, the value of localized targets and the significance of the wider political context are both apparent.

Peter Hain, in his account of the 1969–70 campaign to stop the South African cricket team coming to Britain, uses a number of arguments similar to those invoked by Christabel Pankhurst fifty years earlier. Hain justifies the resort to 'direct action' by the Stop the Seventies Tour campaign as follows:

> STST's direct action tactics—invasions of the field and disruptions, sit-downs, and obstruction of coach journeys, etc.—came under heavy fire. All too often, the more critical refused to view the campaign against the background of sustained lobbying, petitioning

and 'constitutional/normal/peaceful' methods that had characterized the twenty years of work in the campaign for non-racial cricket. . . . The tactics of polite and reasonable persuasion simply had not worked. And it was clear, particularly with cricket and rugby, that they would never work (*Don't Play with Apartheid*, 151).

John Arlott, writing in the *Guardian* on 19 December 1969, also commented: 'The demonstrators, by their action against the rugby tour, have in a few months achieved more than the cricket authorities have done by fifteen years of polite acquiescence' (quoted in ibid., 164).

With the advent of radio and television the importance of publicity has tended to increase. Hain notes that the STST campaign received 'a tremendous amount of publicity', and judges that in view of the threat posed by the demonstrations, the news stories were, on the whole, favourable. The main reasons for the publicity were the novelty of the tactics—direct disruption of matches, and the impression created that more dramatic incidents were due to happen. As a result quite minor protests were reported as part of the overall campaign.

The tactics of the Stop the Tour demonstrators had the immediate effect of embarrassing the authorities trying to ensure the matches were played without disruption—the demonstrators were aided by the inherent difficulties of adequately guarding pitches both prior to and during the matches. Hain writes:

> The threat of direct action also meant that the authorities were forced to over-react. Thus the Wilf Isaacs [rugby] tour, as it neared its completion, was assuming farcical dimensions of busy security. All the tour venues were teeming with policemen and also with suspicious sports authorities (ibid., 124).

A report in *The Times* on 22 May 1970 noted that the cricket grounds for the South African tour matches 'were chosen because of their fortress-like qualities', and looked to the prospect of 'England's best cricket grounds decorated with barbed wire and barriers, and floodlit at night as part of the 24-hour security' (3).

When rugby stewards and the police themselves used rough tactics against protesters this provoked unfavourable comment. After the match at Swansea in November two Labour MPs called for a public enquiry. On 24 November the Home Secretary issued a statement that in future rugby stewards would not be allowed to move demonstrators from the pitch. A former player for Swansea Rugby Club dissociated himself in disgust from the Rugby Union after seeing the behaviour of the rugby stewards. The unsportsman-like behaviour of the stewards probably helped to counter-balance the disruptive role of the demonstrators, and certainly increased publicity. It was after the Swansea match that South

Wales miners decided to support an anti-tour demonstration at an Ebbw Vale match a few days later.

The demonstrations against the rugby tour and the declared aim of trying to prevent the cricket tour roused considerable controversy and strong opposition from those who maintained that 'law and order' must be maintained, that direct action by minorities is intolerant and undemocratic, and by those who wanted to see the games and argued that 'politics should not be brought into sport'. There was some organized opposition to the demonstrators. Thirty well-known personalities were approached by the 1970 Cricket Fund which was appealing for £200,000 to ensure the tour went ahead uninterrupted. The Anti-Demonstration Association issued a statement that 'The South African cricket tour must go on, and we will protect and defend them.' But its threats were never carried into practice. Much more significant was the hostility of some rugby fans. Hain comments that 'the bitterness directed at demonstrators inside the ground by sections of the spectators was often frightening in its venom', and notes that this was shown not only by direct attacks on demonstrators by spectators, but by the cushion throwing at Twickenham which seemed to represent 'the anger of ordinary rugby supporters, who probably would not have gone in for personal skirmishing' (*Don't Play with Apartheid*, 151).

The direct action demonstrations polarized opinion on the issue. Hain points out that the amount of support for them amongst the public was debatable:

> Most of the polls put anti-tour support at between 30 per cent and 40 per cent. But the figures varied according to the way the questions were phrased. Probably the most technically accurate poll of all, conducted by the Social and Community Planning Research just before the cancellation, had its findings reported in the *Guardian* on 20 May. It showed 58 per cent for cancellation, with 53 per cent against asking the white South Africans to Britain in the first place (ibid., 201).

The demonstrators achieved success partly because they managed to win influential recruits. For example, the cricket correspondent of the *Daily Telegraph*, E. W. Swanton, and former England captain Ted Dexter, both swung over to opposing the cricket tour. On 24 May 1970 the *Observer* noted in a survey of the reasons for the final decision to cancel the tour: 'There has certainly been a great change of mind, not only in the Press Box—even among loyal reporters from Tory papers— but also in the ranks of professional cricket' (2). The final cancellation of the tour was due in part to the very real threat of disruption which the demonstrators were able to pose. During the rugby tour over 50,000 demonstrators required 20,000 police on duty at a stated cost of £50,000;

over 400 arrests were made; one match was abandoned and two were switched to new grounds. The delegates at a Police Federation meeting cheered the news that the Home Secretary had asked the Cricket Council to cancel the tour. The chairman of the Federation expressed concern that 'a lot of our people were likely to get injured' (ibid.). But the police also emphasized that if necessary they could manage to contain the demonstrations.

However, the success of the campaign did not lie primarily in its disruptiveness and its threat of greater disorders, but in the fact that its cause commanded widespread and influential support. On 21 April the British Council of Churches called on Christians to join peaceful demonstrations against apartheid in sport, and expressed understanding of the reasons for use of non-violent direct action. A representative of the Baptist Union spoke in favour of methods like flashing mirrors, sounding horns, or releasing rabbits on to a pitch. The same day fifty-one Labour and Liberal MPs tabled a motion that the visit of a team selected on a racial basis was an insult to Commonwealth citizens in Britain. On 2 May Edward Boyle, the former Conservative spokesman on education, became one of two vice-chairmen of the newly launched Fair Cricket Campaign committed to work for a cancellation of the tour in order to minimize the damage to Commonwealth relations and race relations inside Britain. On 9 May a second Conservative MP joined the Fair Cricket Campaign.

The question of reporting on the tour also became an issue among journalists. John Arlott decided not to broadcast for the BBC on the tour. The central London branch of the National Union of Journalists supported a move from the magazine and book branch at the NUJ annual conference urging a boycott of reporting on the tour. The two branches comprise one third of the union's membership, but the resolution was defeated on the grounds that journalists should not embrace self-censorship.

Moreover, the Labour government itself was opposed to the tour, and its initial hesitation over direct intervention was overcome by wider political considerations. Thirteen African countries threatened in April to withdraw from the Commonwealth Games unless the tour was cancelled, and later other Commonwealth countries issued similar threats. The Stop the Seventies Tour campaign was actively enlisting immigrant support for its demonstrations, and by 10 May, according to a spokesman from the Fair Cricket Campaign, a few members of the Cricket Council were beginning to think seriously about possible damage to race relations. A third important consideration was the planned June election. According to *The Times*'s correspondents: 'Some Conservative MPs argued that . . . if there are serious disturbances over the tour during the general election campaign they will react unfavourably on Labour's chances at the poll' (20 May 1970, 1). The chairman of the Institute of Race Relations who urged a last minute cancellation on the Cricket Council, asserted that 'It would have been sheer madness to have had the tour in an election atmosphere.'

The direct action demonstrators could claim a considerable victory—especially as the campaign in Britain provided a model for future protests against South African teams visiting Australia and New Zealand, and was therefore one step in applying international pressure against the practice of apartheid in sport. But the use of direct action was primarily a catalyst within a favourable political context which, by dramatizing the issue and creating a sense of urgency, was able to mobilize sufficient support in favour of stopping the tour. If success had not been achieved prior to the cricket tour it is possible that the demonstrators would have been driven by the logic of their strategy to increasing emphasis on disruption.

The pressures towards increasing 'militancy' emerge from Hain's account of the campaign. After Swansea 'there was a definite feeling of anger and confusion in the air; demonstrators were bitter at having seen their friends wantonly beaten and there was talk of retaliation' (*Don't Play with Apartheid*, 134). The press also highlighted the most disruptive events. Hain comments:

> Our principal quarrel with the press lay in their treatment of the effect of the demonstrations. If the demonstrators succeeded in disrupting a match, then it would be 'hundreds of screaming protesters ran on to the field but were soon cleared off by gallant policemen', but if there were no disruptions . . . then it would be a case of 'the police won'. If the demonstration outside was big, but peaceful, it would get only a brief mention; but if it was rowdy and violent, it would get banner headline coverage—with an editorial inside condemning such protests. This made it extremely difficult to justify the continued use of our nonviolent strategy (ibid., 160).

He also notes that: 'One of our failures . . . was that the public distinction between militant non-violence and violence became very blurred' (ibid., 200).

But not only the brevity of the campaign favoured peaceful militancy. The demonstrators had great tactical advantages, since disrupting a match does not require large numbers and matches provided local targets. A premium was put on imagination and ingenuity. The demonstrations at the matches did not therefore require the massive and long-term support required for a boycott of South African goods or for trade union refusal to make or handle arms destined for South Africa. Moreover, they seemed to have much more impact at the level of publicity and political controversy, which promoted further enthusiasm. Finally, compared with the long-term aims of economic sanctions through a boycott, or of altering British industrial and governmental policy on arms deliveries, stopping the tour was a limited, immediate and achievable goal—factors which greatly contributed to its momentum.

Direct action against the bomb

The direct action movement within the Campaign for Nuclear Disarmament in Britain—which had an ambitious and long-term goal—illustrates the points already made about direct action, and suggests further considerations. The closest parallel is with the Suffragette campaign. Direct action took place within the context of a wider movement committed to constitutional methods, and the campaign continued over a series of years. The role of direct action methods within the campaign continues to be controversial. Unlike the Suffragettes, the activists in the CND could not claim that constitutional methods had been tried and failed, but Bertrand Russell refers to 'long experience' leading to the belief that law-abiding methods alone would not promote a movement capable of enforcing a change in government policy (in Urquhart (ed.), *A Matter of Life*, 194). An assessment of the radical nature of the goal of unilateral nuclear disarmament also led to the conviction that it would not be carried through by any British government unless there was strong popular opposition to the bomb to counter-balance military and political interests committed to nuclear strategy, and to reverse orthodox government attitudes to 'defence'. Marxists and anarchists argued that the bomb symbolized the evils of the existing system and that disarmament required a fundamental change in economic and political organization.

Whether or not these assessments were realistic depends not only on one's view of British politics, but also on the actual goal of the CND—which was itself a matter of some ambiguity. It is arguable that if the goal was only the abandonment of the British independent deterrent, then this had become politically and strategically realistic by 1962 when the United States was anxious to be the only nuclear power in the West, and to discourage British and French ambitions to nuclear independence. By this time the economic difficulties of keeping up with missile technology had also made themselves apparent. Moreover, the CND was always able to make out a strong case that Britain was too small and too densely populated to make the risk of becoming a direct nuclear target a rational choice, even within the parameters of strategic definitions of rationality. For the first two or three years of the campaign the dangers from nuclear tests and the need to give up the British bomb were the main focus of CND policy. However, the moral and political logic of the CND's opposition to nuclear weapons led the campaign formally to argue that unilateral disarmament entailed withdrawal from NATO so long as it remained primarily dependent on atomic weapons and on the US strategic H-bomb force. A policy of 'positive neutralism' which meant renouncing the pattern of

foreign policy since the Second World War, altering relationships with
the United States, and threatening the 'balance of power' in western
Europe, clearly did signify a much more radical change of policy, and
hence, one much harder to achieve either through constitutional means or
direct action in the context of the existing party and parliamentary system.
Supporters of direct action came increasingly to favour attempts at
comprehensive social change as a necessary aspect of the movement
against the bomb.

Arguments in favour of direct action tended, however, to focus on a
simpler issue: the extreme urgency of taking action to avert the threat of
nuclear war. For example, this was the main point made by the *New
Statesman* commenting editorially on an attempt to obstruct the building
of a Thor missile base in Norfolk in December 1958. This argument
assumed that direct action was in some sense more effective than purely
constitutional means.

The most popular reason for favouring direct action—especially among
its sympathizers in the ranks of the CND—was that it gained wide press
and media coverage. Bertrand Russell also argued that the publicity
accruing from mass sit-downs and obstruction of nuclear bases was the
main justification for these methods: 'By means of civil disobedience a
certain kind of publicity becomes possible. . . . Many people are roused to
enquire into questions which they had been willing to ignore' (ibid.,
193–4).

The publicity value of direct action was however probably less
important to the CND campaign than it was to the suffrage movement.
The CND and the issue of nuclear disarmament were for several years
regarded as newsworthy by virtue of their political significance—and the
moves towards supporting unilateralism among the trade unions in 1959
and 1960, and the struggle in the Labour Party in 1961 increased this
significance. Whilst civil disobedience demonstrations certainly were
news, they gained in newsworthiness by being part of the wider campaign.

Second, the political impact of publicity was different. The Suffragettes demonstrated their determination to win the vote, which in
principle parliament had often conceded to be a justified demand. The
demonstrators at missile or submarine bases, on the other hand, were
trying to persuade people to take one side in a new, controversial and
complicated political debate about deterrence and defence, and to bring
about a fundamental change in attitude to traditional government conceptions of defence policy. The persuasive power of direct action was seen
therefore primarily to lie in publicizing the realities behind abstract
theories of deterrence—the missiles and bombs ready for use. Civil
disobedience could also be seen as a means of penetrating the screen of
security—supposed secrecy about the location of missile bases, or the
revelation of previously secret government policy: like the existence of

underground regional seats of government to come into use in the event of a nuclear war.

In confrontations with the authorities the direct actionists (like the Suffragettes) initially won great sympathy, especially within the ranks of the CND, when they were sentenced to brief terms in jail. Over the years, increasingly severe sentences tended to bring diminishing returns in publicity and sympathy—though when Bertrand Russell went to jail for a week in September 1961, he was accorded worldwide news coverage. Like the Suffragettes the demonstrators were able, up to a point, to use the courts as a forum for stating their political views on the bomb—especially when six members of the Committee of 100 were tried in 1962 on conspiracy charges arising out of a demonstration at the Wethersfield H-bomber base. One of the six, defending himself at the Old Bailey, forced a prosecution witness, Air Commodore McGill, to admit that he would if necessary 'press the button' to start a nuclear attack.

In the confrontations with the authorities the police often tried to neutralize their effect by tolerating sit-downs, or by carefully carrying away demonstrators. The disadvantages of allowing demonstrators to be man-handled were illustrated by the wide publicity given to the first direct action demonstration at a Norfolk missile base, when labourers on the site were encouraged to attack demonstrators, and the police left the RAF to deal with the protesters. Left-wing Labour MPs asked questions about the treatment of the demonstrators, whilst Conservative MPs asked how they were able to get inside what was meant to be a top-security base. At a follow-up demonstration two weeks later the police carried protesters away with great care, whilst a largely sympathetic corps of journalists watched for any evidence of ill treatment.

The government ran into greatest trouble with the Committee of 100 when, after allowing two mass sit-downs to take place in the centre of London (on the first occasion there were no arrests), they banned in September 1961 a rally in Trafalgar Square which was to have been the prelude to a big sit-down, and arrested one-third of the Committee members in advance. The banning of the Trafalgar Square meeting under the Defence of the Realm Act immediately turned the demonstration into a civil liberties issue. About 12,000 people converged on the Square—compared with an estimated 5,000 on the previous Committee of 100 demonstration in April—either to defy the ban, or as spectators. Thousands sat down. The police became increasingly rough in handling the demonstrators, especially after midnight, and as a result evoked hostile press comment.

Direct action in the CND created some of the difficulties that militancy had posed for the women's suffrage movement. The constitutional leaders feared direct action would alienate public opinion and distract attention from their own efforts. There were organizational conflicts between the Direct Action Committee and the executive of the CND, and a more serious, and publicized, split between the chairman of the CND and Bertrand Russell, when Russell initiated the Committee of 100 in 1960. These clashes arose, however, over organizational control of the movement as well as over methods. Among CND supporters at large, direct action was usually seen as a useful complement to the more orthodox methods. Mrs Fawcett's comments on the votes for women campaign provide a parallel: 'however acute were the differences between the heads of the different societies, the general mass of suffragists throughout the country were loyal to the cause by whomsoever it was represented' (*Women's Suffrage*, 61-2).

The impact on the public of direct action against the bomb is difficult to assess. Frank Parkin states in his book *Middle Class Radicalism* that with the advent of the Committee of 100, opinion polls showed a decline in support for unilateralism. But apart from the limitations of poll questions in elucidating attitudes to complex policies like unilateralism, other political factors may have been as, or more, important in shaping opinion: for example, press support for Mr Gaitskell in his determination to reverse the 1960 Labour Party Conference decision in favour of British unilateral nuclear disarmament. Moreover, although Gallup Poll questions indicated a percentage drop in support for unilateralism in September 1961, another Gallup survey the same month indicated a percentage increase in general anxiety about nuclear weapons. Christopher Driver concludes: 'The peak of public concern seems to have been September 1961, the month of reaction to renewal of Russian and American H-bomb tests, and of the Committee of 100's Trafalgar Square sit-down' (*The Disarmers*, 98).*

In examining how far the direct action demonstrations against nuclear weapons promoted a tendency to increasing militancy it is necessary to distinguish between the Direct Action Committee which was active (in slightly varying organizational guises) between 1957 and 1961, and the Committee of 100 which held its first demonstration in February 1961. The Direct Action Committee was committed to a long term strategy of non-co-operation and resistance centred on the various specific aspects of nuclear strategy—nuclear weapon production and the nuclear bases. In aid of this strategy they appealed to workers at Aldermaston atomic

---

* The Gallup Poll findings on the response to the question: 'Would you approve or disapprove if Britain gave up her H-bombs even if other countries did not do so?' were as follows:

	April 1958	Sept. 1958	March 1959	Sept. 1961	Dec. 1961	April 1962
Approve	25	30	30	21	31	22
Disapprove	61	57	50	62	55	64
Don't know	14	13	20	17	14	14

plant to leave their jobs, tried to persuade local trade unions to black building work and supplies to missile bases, and urged strike action in firms concentrating on bomber or missile production. They also tried to mobilize local opinion in general against nuclear bases or weapon production.

These activities were supplemented by much better-publicized demonstrations—attempts to enter nuclear testing areas, to obstruct work on missile bases or to hinder the operations of Polaris submarines. These demonstrations were intended partly to symbolize the potential for obstruction if sit-downs or physical entry into a nuclear zone were carried out on a mass scale, partly to demonstrate the potentialities of non-violent resistance in contrast with the paraphernalia of nuclear strategy, and partly to dramatize the urgency of the nuclear peril and the depth of concern of the demonstrators.

Demonstrations were explicitly based on adherence to a Gandhian theory of non-violence. Whilst this was due primarily to the commitments of the organizers, a strategy of explicit non-violence was also dictated by the desire to avoid alienating public opinion. After the political quiescence of the 1950s, any illegal demonstration appeared extremely militant. Press treatment which tended to emphasize sensational and disruptive aspects magnified any violence. The first missile base demonstration was headlined by some papers as a 'riot', and the fact that demonstrators entering the base crushed rolls of barbed wire—the cost was estimated at £200—was stressed. By the time of the anti-tour actions eleven years later this scale of damage would scarcely be noticeable.

The Committee of 100 was founded in an attempt to increase the numbers of people taking part in civil disobedience, so that direct action was moved away from the image of individual witness and into the stage of mass resistance. Its first three demonstrations were held in central London. Whilst this was partly for tactical reasons—to increase the likelihood of large numbers—it also suggested a much more direct challenge to the government, and a more directly-disruptive intention. In its long-term aims the Committee of 100 was more explicitly insurrectionary. It was also more militant in tone than the Direct Action Committee —more willing to consider sabotage as a tactic, less willing to practise Gandhian 'civil disobedience'. Nevertheless, in practice the Committee maintained a strategy of non-violence.

The Committee of 100 never faced the dilemma of 'mild militancy' being played out, because before the full range of non-violent tactics had been tried, the Committee had already begun to lose momentum. To some extent the Committee shared in the general decline of the movement for nuclear disarmament due to a sense that the dangers from nuclear weapons had been reduced (especially after the Partial Test Ban Treaty of 1963) and disillusionment with the possibility of achieving a direct change in government policy. However, the Committee's support began to decline sooner and faster than that of the broader campaign. This was due much more specifically to the fact that the authorities, by imposing prison sentences of one year to eighteen months on six leading members of the Committee, achieved a deterrent effect—especially as the Committee failed to mount a direct challenge to the conspiracy trial of some of its key members. The larger numbers, and much of the eminent support for the Committee, had been won on the basis that there was safety in numbers, and when this belief was disproved, the less committed supporters withdrew.

Nevertheless, the Committee of 100 mounted a series of major demonstrations at nuclear bases after the conspiracy trial, and there was a further more interesting reason for its avoidance of a strategy of increasing disruption. This was due to the beliefs of many Committee members, and to the anarchist tendencies inherent in commitment to direct action. The Committee began consciously to broaden its objectives to include action for radical social change at many levels—it undertook, for example, an early demonstration about the problem of homeless families at the Newington Lodge hostel in London. In line with this new policy scope, and with its ethos favouring direct democracy, the Committee also undertook an extensive reorganization which involved decentralizing itself into a number of regional committees—a move which probably strengthened the tendency to look to action on more localized issues. In fact, some of the most active members of the Committee of 100 moved on to become prominent in the squatters' campaigns and in community organizing.

It is, however, possible to argue that the Committee of 100 paved the way for the explicit commitment to violent 'direct action' of the Vietnam movement which grew up in 1967 and 1968. It is certainly true that since CND and the Committee of 100 were seen to have failed, their methods were also seen as weak and ineffective. Arguably, the nuclear disarmament movement succeeded in arousing public concern, and in posing a serious political challenge, and its failure was due in part to the inherent difficulties of achieving the goal of a neutral Britain. But in the eyes of the new student radicals, the CND was undoubtedly a failure. It also seems that the precedent of direct action and disobedience of the law set by the nuclear disarmament protesters paved the way for later movements—the Stop the Tour demonstrations, for example, took place in a context where, on the Left, direct action was regarded as a normal tactic. But the militancy of the students of the late 1960s stemmed from quite distinct political causes. One important cause of frustration on the Left lay in the policies of the Labour government—in particular its failure to oppose the American war in Vietnam. Indeed, it was the coming to power of the Labour government in 1964, with an apparent commitment to give up the independent British bomb, which finally demonstrated the political impotence of the

CND. (Though the CND's inability to work effectively through the Labour Party was shown in 1961 when the unilateralist decision was reversed.) Many prominent Labour Party members of the CND were co-opted into the new government, others left the campaign. When the new government quietly continued the defence policy of its predecessor, few CND members within the Party made any protest, and the direct action movement, which had always been deeply suspicious of working through the Labour Party, no longer existed to pose even a minor challenge.

The other reasons for student militancy in the late 1960s were of international inspiration: the growing prestige of guerrilla warfare and tendency to identify with the Liberation Front in Vietnam; the examples of student activity, in West Germany and especially in France in May 1968; and above all, a tendency to follow the trends of the anti-war and anti-racialist movements in the United States.

From civil rights to Black Power

Consideration of the evolution of the civil rights movement from committed non-violence to the slogan of 'Black Power' and support for urban guerrilla warfare is both illuminating in itself and important in its wider effects on other movements.

In its early stages the civil rights struggle had much greater political advantages than any of the campaigns considered so far, even though it involved much greater personal risk; and it also achieved more far-reaching success. The legitimacy of the protesters' cause was, outside the South, almost universally recognized. The legitimacy of direct action methods was more controversial. According to national opinion polls throughout the 1960s there was roughly a two-to-one majority among whites against the sit-ins, the freedom rides, the Washington rally in 1963 and the voter-registration project in Mississippi in 1964. (It is interesting that by 1963 the differences of attitude between the North and the South were declining (see Skolnick (ed.), *The Politics of Protest*, 186).) But it was possible to make out a strong case that sit-ins, freedom rides and the defiance of local police orders were an assertion of basic constitutional rights. The demonstrations achieved nationwide, and often worldwide, publicity, dramatized the injustice and brutality of segregation and demonstrated the new determination of the younger generation. Bob Moses, who became active in the Student Non-violent Co-ordinating Committee, commented on the first sit-ins: 'The students in that picture had a certain look on their faces, sort of sullen, angry, determined. Before, the Negro in the South had always looked on the defensive, cringing. This time they were taking the initiative' (quoted in Zinn, *SNCC: The New Abolitionists*, 17).

Above all, direct action for civil rights seemed in the period 1956–64 to be outstandingly successful. It was successful in winning many localized campaigns—against segregation on the buses, in restaurants and drug stores, in libraries, parks, swimming pools and churches in many towns. W. Haywood Burns in a study of black protest in America summarizes the position in 1963:

> Since the start of the sit-ins in 1960, the movement has met with increasing success and has involved large numbers of both whites and Negroes. It is estimated that over 200 cities have had some kind of non-violent direct-action protest demonstration; there have been 70,000 visible, direct participants; approximately 6,000 different people have been jailed (*The Voices of Negro Protest in America*, 59).

Non-violent direct action was also successful in either promoting Congressional legislation—which followed the sit-ins, or in ensuring federal enforcement of existing Supreme Court decisions, for example, the desegregation of facilities at terminals for interstate transport. The Birmingham, Alabama campaign in 1963 which was a more comprehensive and militant attempt to change the pattern of desegregation in the town as a whole, and the response by police chief 'Bull' Connor, embarrassed the Kennedy administration into actively promoting the Civil Rights Bill promised in the 1960 election campaign. The political leverage of the civil rights demonstrators was provided not only by the support they commanded in the North (so long as the campaign was restricted to the South) and the administration's verbal commitment to their cause, but also by the embarrassment the United States felt in its role as leader of the 'free world' when American citizens were very visibly being denied their most basic human rights. As black African states began to attain their independence, both the incongruity of segregation and the impatience of black Americans became more pronounced.

The success of direct action was a powerful argument which swung previously hesitant civil rights leaders to support it. Bayard Rustin noted how after the Birmingham campaign of 1963 black leaders of the older organizations had changed their stand:

> For example, Roy Wilkins, executive secretary of the NAACP, who only a year ago, from a platform in Jackson, Mississippi, criticized the direct-action methods of the Freedom Riders, was arrested recently for leading a picket-line in that very city, after hundreds of NAACP members had been arrested in a direct-action struggle (in Goodman (ed.), *Seeds of Liberation*, 318).

Kenneth Clark has also noted how militants and radicals:

> propelled more orderly and stable groups . . . towards increasing

acceptance of direct action methods not only because some of the older leaders found the ardor of youth contagious but also because . . . they sensed that bolder programs would be necessary if their own roles were not to be undermined (in Conant, *The Prospects for Revolution*, 107–8).

The limitations of direct action emerged as it became clearer that progress in essential areas like housing and jobs depended more on radical political changes than on desegregation. But the first impulse of the civil rights campaign was to turn towards organizing black Americans in ways which would make their combined needs felt.

The first important step was the registration of black voters in the South, initiated by the SNCC as early as 1961 parallel to direct action to integrate public facilities. The voter-registration drives in the diehard Southern states of Mississippi, Alabama and South West Georgia reached their peak in the summer of 1964. The political significance of registering black citizens to vote was clear from the statistics. In Mississippi, the most extreme case, about 45 per cent of the population was black, but only 4 per cent had been allowed to register as voters. In Alabama, roughly one-third of its population was black, but only 14 per cent could vote. The awareness of whites of the potential threat from negro votes, especially in the 110 southern counties where they were in the majority, was shown by the state devices adopted to prevent the registration of negroes under the state laws, and by the intimidation and delaying tactics employed to prevent registration. Due to prolonged registration campaigns and accompanying violent reactions, the federal government passed in 1965 the Voting Rights Act abolishing the poll tax as a prerequisite to vote (it had been abolished for federal elections by the 24th Amendment passed in 1964), suspending literacy and other tests designed to hinder registration, and increasing federal powers to prevent discrimination in the registration of negro voters.

The increased power of black voters in the South had some effect in getting black representatives elected. By 1964, prior to the Voting Act, 450,000 black voters had been added to the electoral rolls in the South. Julian Bond, from the SNCC, was elected to the Georgia legislature in 1964, and by 1966, ninety black Americans had been elected to state legislatures, several in the South, and to local offices—even in Mississippi. Over time, the increasing numbers of black voters has also had some effect on the policies of white politicians, who have had to take some notice of this section of their constituency. According to the US Commission on Civil Rights Report published in October 1970, the registration of black voters in Southern states was one area where since 1965 there had been 'dramatic, statistically measurable progress'. But these changes can only be regarded as very limited reforms resulting in only slightly increased influence and bargaining power of black Americans within the party system, Congress and the administration.

A more radical challenge to conventional politics—and in particular to the Democratic Party with its coalition between the trade union, professional and semi-liberal interests of the North with the segregationists of the deep South—was the creation in 1964 of the Mississippi Freedom Democratic Party, which bypassed the state registration system and the all-white Democratic Party machine. It registered its own voters, and organized state-wide conventions at county, and then Congressional district, level to send delegates to the Democratic Party Convention in August, and to claim the seats accorded to the traditional all-white delegation from Mississippi. The Freedom Party which caused some embarrassment to the managers and candidates of the Democratic Party, nevertheless found support on the Credentials Committee, and was offered a weak compromise to seat two of its delegates. The FDP rejected it, and staged a sit-in at the Convention in the Mississippi seats. After the 1964 elections the FDP promoted a challenge to the seating of the five Mississippi Congressmen in the House of Representatives, on the grounds that their election was invalid. Three women who had polled high votes in unofficial Freedom elections for Congress tried to enter the House to take up their seats. The FDP case was supported by 149 Congressmen, but 276 voted against them and ensured the Mississippi regulars kept their seats. Howard Zinn comments: 'This was a new kind of politics the FDP was engaging in, something that might be called *protest politics*, because it exerted its force both *against* and *within* the traditional politics' (*SNCC: The New Abolitionists*, 261).

The fact that the Democratic Party was prepared in the interests of keeping Southern votes to conciliate the whites from Mississippi in preference to the Freedom Democratic Party led to disillusionment with the idea of 'coalition' with white groups. Carmichael and Hamilton wrote:

> It is absolutely imperative that black people strive to form an independent base of political power *first*. When they can control their own communities—however large or small—then other groups will make overtures to them based on a wise calculation of self-interest (*Black Power*, 96).

The successor to the Mississippi Freedom Party was the Lowndes County Freedom Organization, created in March 1966, in a county in Alabama with an 81 per cent black population and a diehard white minority. The aim of the Lowndes Organization was to create an independent third party, and it ran its own slate of candidates for the county elections in November 1966.

The logic of creating independent bases of political power applied equally strongly to the black ghettos of the North. As Carmichael and

Hamilton noted, the black vote in the mid-1960s held the balance in many cities, and within twenty years there was likely to be a black majority in a dozen major cities. But political voting power needed to be supplemented by internal community control and some degree of economic independence. Carmichael and Hamilton called for parent boards which would take control of the ghetto schools; tenant unions which would force slum landlords to repair their property, or else would take it over completely; and pressure on merchants to re-invest about half their profits in the ghettos, with boycotts of those who refused. CORE, one of the main civil rights bodies, was by 1964 already turning to ghetto organizing, and by 1966 the theme of Black Power had been accepted at the CORE annual convention.

Black Power was one way of moving on from direct action to exerting political power. The alternative strategy, embraced by some direct action leaders like Bayard Rustin, was to work within the system, especially the Democratic Party, and to seek change through a policy of political coalition. This approach meant regarding direct action as a means of rousing publicity and prodding a reluctant Congress and Administration into action—as one avenue towards reform rather than as a radical alternative to existing policies. The Black Power conception, on the other hand, meant taking many elements inherent in direct action towards their logical political conclusions—creating a power base outside the established political bodies, promoting community action, challenging the conventional policies and manoeuvres of the political parties, and so trying to avoid the dangers of co-optation and premature compromise.

That Black Power became associated with violence rather than with political strategy based on community organization was due to a number of factors. The paranoid white reaction to the challenge of black independence, which translated Black Power into black violence, was aided by press exaggeration and stereotypes. The link with violence was probably associatively enhanced by the riots in 1964, 1965 and 1966 in the city ghettos. It was also given some substance by the fact that the turn towards Black Power was linked to conscious and vocal repudiation of the Martin Luther King brand of non-violence—coming to be associated with crawling humility and cowardly passivity—and with avowed approval of the doctrine of armed self-defence. Thus far, Black Power could be seen to be acting within the American tradition, which had endorsed the right of resistance to tyranny, written into the constitution the right to bear arms, and created as its folk hero the cowboy, gun on hip, quick-on-the-draw to defend his honour and to avenge injustices. Claiming the right to fight back is, in this perspective, primarily a more aggressive assertion of the overall demand for equality. Truman Nelson commented in his introductory essay to Robert F. Williams's case for self-defence, *Negroes with Guns*: 'The American negro is a citizen in a rich land, with a citizen's rights and duty to resist; *resist* all attempts to deprive him of its manifold blessings' (*Nation*, 22 April 1968, 543).

Then after a brief period in which Black Power was misrepresented as a strategy based on violence, exponents and supporters of Black Power began to talk and act in a way which made this equation half real. By 1967 Carmichael was forecasting guerrilla warfare based in the urban ghettos. The Black Panther Party, created as a self-defence organization, combined demands for black independence with a very visible expression of their willingness to fight for it by wearing guns.

It is not difficult to find psychological reasons for militant blacks espousing violence—a natural expression of released rage after years of suffering from overt and covert racial prejudice and discrimination; a response to the way American society has emasculated the image and self-image of the black man, whilst holding up a counter-image of aggressive white virility; and the associated determination to fight back at white society whatever the cost. There are also important sociological considerations. Direct action campaigns in the South relied either on student volunteers, or on settled local communities, and were organizationally focused on the local churches. Militance in the ghetto involved especially the jobless and frustrated 'young bloods' that Carmichael pins his hopes on, possessed of a much more reckless anger, and in the forefront of the riots. Whilst the riots in the mid-1960s certainly had political overtones even when they erupted spontaneously in response to local police provocation (for example the riots following the assassination of King had purely political origins), their political significance was greatly enhanced by the wider context of previous civil rights agitation. Unlike the highly organized non-violent action in the South, riots had occurred before in the urban slums, and can be seen in part as a product of those conditions.

But it is most profitable to concentrate on specifically political factors, which encouraged resort to violent protest. First, the policies pursued by the federal government played an important role in embittering its black citizens. The roles of the Justice Department and the FBI are particularly important. Despite the fact that the Attorney General, Robert Kennedy, initiated a much more serious attempt to enforce federal laws on desegregation in the South than the previous administration—which had done nothing, his efforts still appeared negligible to the Negroes in the South, and especially to the committed civil rights campaigners. It was noted by a number of observers that the FBI showed a marked reluctance to take action against Southern law officers who brutally assaulted blacks. I. F. Stone commented:

The Department of Justice has not been too energetic in civil rights cases, for these bring it into conflict with the Southern oligarchy in

Congress. . . . There has not been a conviction in a police brutality case, white or colored, for more than two years, since October 30, 1959, though more than 1300 complaints were received and 52 prosecutions authorized in the two and a half years from January, 1958 to July, 1960 (*In a Time of Torment*, 142–3).

Despite a number of federal measures designed to promote better housing, education and job opportunities, the government has failed to make much progress even in those areas where it has direct influence. Justice Douglas writing in 1970 notes:

> The federal government, with its hundreds of federally-financed public road contracts, and its thousands of procurement contracts negotiated each year by the Pentagon and other agencies . . . is admonished by Congress to make sure that the contractors for these goods make jobs available without discrimination. President Johnson gave hardly more than lip service to that mandate (*Points of Rebellion*, 45–6).

The 1970 Civil Rights Commission strongly criticized the poor progress made in providing equal employment and housing opportunities, which it ascribed to the 'failure to provide overall co-ordination and direction to the entire Federal civil rights effort'. A brief attempt was made by President Johnson in 1965 to set up a Council on Equal Opportunities under the Vice-President, but it was abandoned after a few months when its efforts created trouble with other government departments and agencies. Moreover, the Justice Department, which was given the co-ordinating role, made very little attempt to use the enforcement clause in the 1964 Act entitling the government to cut off funds to any source that fostered discrimination. The report found that use of this clause became 'increasingly peripheral' to the work of the Department. Second, the more far-reaching aims of promoting economic and social equality, compared with the symbolic equality of desegregation, demanded greater patience, greater political resources, and were less likely to meet with visible successes. The fact that Black Power was turning from the South to the North meant that it no longer met such easy sympathy there and was exposing the superficiality of Northern liberalism. This switch in emphasis also encouraged a more radical critique of the American economy and American society—racialism came to be seen as part of the whole structure of American society.

Anger with the federal government, and determination to reject all the values and institutions of white America, were greatly increased by the Vietnam War. The ruthlessness of the military methods used against an Asian people were seen as proof of its contempt for the lives or rights of non-whites. Black leaders also noted that in proportion to the population as a whole, a disproportionate number of black soldiers were sent to Vietnam, and a disproportionate number also died there, because they were sent into the field to fight rather than securing the safer and more prestigious jobs in the background. Moreover, the war underlined the irony of the fact that black Americans were killing Vietnamese, allegedly in the name of freedom, whilst they did not enjoy their own freedom at home.

At a SNCC conference in May 1966, the 130 members who attended decided that the SNCC would not take part in a White House Conference on civil rights, because 'the executive department and the President are not serious about insuring Constitutional rights to black Americans' and because the SNCC could not 'in good conscience meet with the chief policy maker of the Vietnam war' when he was flagrantly violating the rights of Vietnamese. The chairman of the SNCC, John Lewis, who decided personally to take part in the conference, was replaced by Stokely Carmichael. The mood of the conference was indicated by the rejection of integration as a goal, and by Carmichael's announcement to the press that Black Panther candidates would be 'protected by the toughest Negroes we can find in Watts, Harlem, Chicago and Washington' (in Segal, *America's Receding Future*, 258).

The Vietnam war had a further effect—it strongly suggested that the American government was prepared, when its interests were seriously threatened, to resort to unlimited violence in order to maintain them. The continuing political and military success of the NLF and North Vietnamese, despite the American saturation-bombing, also suggested that a committed and sustained guerrilla struggle could defeat American power. Identification with and admiration for the Vietnamese encouraged a tendency to think in terms of waging guerrilla war on the home front— and the war itself was radicalizing numbers of the soldiers who fought in it and ensuring they went home psychologically and physically trained for military struggle.

Vietnam and student militance

The Vietnam war had a decisive impact not only on the Black Power movement, but also on the white radical movements in the United States—and by extension in Europe. It is interesting, for example, that the moves by the Students for a Democratic Society towards ghetto and community organizing were largely interrupted by the urgent requirements of opposition to the Vietnam war. The mounting violence of the American military in Vietnam also encouraged polarization between government and opposition at home, so the opposition tended to express increasing solidarity with the Vietnamese guerrillas. Moreover, the role of the State Department and the CIA in South Vietnam, the profits reaped by business corporations like Dow Chemicals from the war, the deep involvement of many of the most prestigious universities in research designed to help the government win the war, and the well-documented dishonesty of American propaganda on Vietnam all contributed to make it a symbol of the militarism and economic imperialism of America.

Both the intensity of the Vietnam war and its encouragement to protesters to take up a committed opposition to American and western imperialism required demonstrators to show a greater urgency and militancy. This expressed itself in support for violent methods of resistance. These tendencies were reflected in the British demonstrations against Vietnam in the late 1960s, for example, in advocacy of the October 1968 demonstration. Peter Buckman argued in the *Black Dwarf* that demonstrations should not be seen as 'single issue campaigns' but 'as part of a mounting campaign against the system and all it stands for' (in Halloran *et al.*, *Demonstrations and Communications*, 67). Another writer in the CND newspaper declared:

> This is a new type of demonstration. It stems from an increasing recognition that violence is inherent in Western capitalist societies.
> . . . Violence is proclaimed by a situation where power is unequally distributed and decisions are made by a minority 'up there' and passed down through authority (ibid., 67–8).

The same author commented: 'This then is no peace march; its militancy flows from the . . . identification with a revolutionary struggle in Vietnam.'

Whilst the importance of the war in influencing protest movements can scarcely be exaggerated, its full impact has to be understood in conjunction with the political context in the middle and late 1960s. The disillusionment of the British Left with the policy of the Labour government after 1964 was noted earlier as one factor making for greater militancy and a tendency to look towards extra-constitutional methods. But the Labour Party does have genuine policy differences with the Conservatives, and is influenced by the tradition and egalitarian values of the Labour movement. The trade unions also play a significant role in Labour policy, and although in the 1950s union influence was on many issues towards the Right, by the end of the 1960s on domestic policy in particular, the unions were pushing the Party towards the Left. The possibility of the Labour Party becoming the vehicle of radical and socialist movements is sufficiently great to divide the British Left permanently on the issue of whether to work within or outside the Party.

In the United States, on the other hand, the policy differences between the Republicans and Democrats have often been virtually non-existent, and the slightly more liberal bias of many Democratic Party supporters counter-balanced by the solid Southern bloc and the role of the Party bosses. Moreover, the fact that the ostensibly liberal President Kennedy had countenanced the Bay of Pigs invasion, and involved the USA in the Vietnam War, and that President Johnson's 'moderate' image was designed solely to defeat Goldwater in the 1964 election, disillusioned many who had believed in Party politics. Nevertheless, the numbers of students who flocked to help Senator McCarthy early in 1968 indicated a willingness to turn from direct action to conventional politics, if the latter could be made relevant. The Chicago Convention, which signalled a victory for the Party machine over the stirring of protest both inside the Convention hall and outside on the streets, also turned a number of people towards greater militance.

The significance of the existence of some form of established political opposition is suggested by the evolution of the New Left in West Germany. The period of greatest New Left activity occurred between 1967-9. This coincided with an international tendency to student radicalism, and the American influence was undoubtedly important—Vietnam became a symbol of the system which was to be rejected. But the New Left was also a response to disillusionment with the Social Democratic Party, which in the late 1950s had abandoned its attempt to oppose the cold war and the military policies of the Adenauer regime, and which had watered down its domestic policies. Just prior to the 1969 elections the *Frank-furter Allgemeine Zeitung* explained to its readers that to understand Swedish politics they must realize that the Swedish Christian Democrats were to the left of the SPD in Germany. And it is probably not irrelevant that in the period 1967-9 the Social Democrats had gone into coalition with the Christian Democrats, so that there was no parliamentary opposition in an even formal sense. After Brandt took office in 1969 a number of former SDS members welcomed his Öst-Politik.

In addition to the question of whether or not a genuine parliamentary opposition exists, the degree to which the political system as a whole, or key individual political leaders, can command respect is also liable to affect radical attitudes. In Italy, for example, the Communist Party provides a stable opposition—though it is perhaps too effectively isolated from wielding political power, except at a local level. But Italian citizens have a well-founded scepticism about the possibility of any government promoting serious internal reforms in view of the shifting parliamentary coalitions, and bureaucratic inefficiency and corruption. In strongly authoritarian or hopelessly corrupt regimes, radical dissidents are likely to turn to guerrilla warfare and not simply to sporadic violent demonstrations.

Many Americans have become increasingly disillusioned about promoting serious reforms through the administration—for example, relieving the plight of the very poor or overcoming discrimination in employment. They have also become convinced that foreign and military policy is dictated by powerful business and defence organizations which are not amenable to political control. But cynicism has been increased by the sense that elected presidents have deliberately misled Congress and the public over the Vietnam war, disguising moves towards escalation by offers of negotiations, and covering up the bombing and shooting of civilians. Deep distrust of administration policy has manifested itself in the Senate since the mid-1960s. Whilst growing Senate opposition to the Vietnam war may for a time have fostered belief in the possibility of effective action through the conventional political channels, the conduct of the Nixon administration—for example, sending troops into Cambodia, turned the movement against the war towards violent militancy.

A *Guardian* article on student unrest at Madison university on 14 May 1970, reported that 'More than twenty buildings have been fire-bombed, but only one burned to the ground. . . . On top of the fire damage shop window "trashing"—running down a street lobbing bricks through the windows—has caused damage amounting to several thousand pounds.' The reporter quoted a moderate student leader:

> We've tried peaceful means of stopping this war for five years.
> It doesn't work. The blacks tried peaceful means of ending their
> poverty. It didn't work. Rioting brought the blacks more poverty
> money; we hope rioting will bring us peace. . . . We have to be
> violent to get on the news screen (2).

This statement sums up the tendencies towards increasing violence which may arise when established political methods appear hopelessly inadequate, peaceful direct action has not achieved success, and when the urgency of the issue and sense of frustration preclude long-term forms of community and political organization outside the established parties. These conditions are most likely to apply to protests against foreign and military policy—especially where there is an ongoing war; and least likely to be operative where direct action is used locally to gain limited goals, like housing homeless families. The following chapter considers whether the assumption that violence is more effective than peaceful protest is justified.

4 Violence and power

The preceding chapter suggested that the resort to violence might be a recognition of relative powerlessness, rather than an expression of power. Our tendency to equate power with violence is thus an oversimplification. It is therefore worth examining the idea put forward by Hannah Arendt in her study *On Violence* that 'power' and 'violence' should be understood as polar opposites.

The distinction she makes between the two categories is relevant to an understanding of direct action and the strategy of protest movements. In her definition power arises out of the combined action of large numbers of people. A mass demonstration is therefore a show of potential power. Mass direct action which involves some degree of economic coercion, as in strikes and boycotts, is an exercise in power. So is mass non-co-operation or civil disobedience which hampers or burdens the administrative machinery of government. Miss Arendt specifically cites the non-violent civil rights struggle as an expression of power.

While power arises out of social co-operation, violence is seen by Miss Arendt as an instrument which can be wielded by a small minority. Pure violence does not require large numbers of people—a machine gun, bomb or hand grenade can be handled by one or two men. Terror, the psychological counterpart of violent acts, can also be promoted by a few.

However, the ambiguity of the term 'violence' requires that this clear-cut distinction should be modified. There are, for example, forms of popular 'violence' which may occur, or be threatened, which do not rely primarily on the technical efficiency of weapons, but are expressions of a movement manifesting its combined power. One example is mob action and rioting, which indicate either a semi-political but largely unorganized form of mass demonstration, or the spilling over of anger and frustration by a more articulate movement.

At the other end of the scale is disciplined, mass armed resistance, and spontaneous insurrection. The success of an insurrection may depend more on the extent of its support than on the sophistication of its weapons, and on the amount of sympathy for the rebels within the armed forces. The Russian Revolution occurred in 1917 partly because many of the army supported the revolution. An insurrection is distinct from a *coup d'état*, which depends on the military efficiency of the conspirators and the military advantage of surprise.

Another form of popular violence falls between spontaneous rioting and actual insurrection; that is, street fighting and the resort to the barricades. This kind of confrontation with the police or army occasionally develops out of street demonstrations, as it did in Paris in May 1968. But erecting barricades as a prelude to insurrection is typical of nineteenth-century rather than twentieth-century attempts at revolution. The 'ideal type' of revolution in the second half of this century is guerrilla warfare.

The concept of 'guerrilla' tactics is itself by no means unambiguous. Any bomb explosion, shooting incident, kidnapping or hijacking carried out by a group with political grievances tends to come under this rubric. But in some cases acts of violence by small groups—like the Angry Brigade in Britain, or the Baader-Meinhof group in Germany—are more reminiscent of the anarchist 'propaganda by deed' than of a genuine guerrilla movement. A guerrilla image may also be extended to a group which sees armed violence as a means of defence against the authorities, but not as a strategy of revolution, as in the case of the Black Panthers. Guerrilla warfare requires popular support, even if this support stems from a minority group; and contemporary guerrilla activity (as opposed to the older form of partisan warfare against an occupying military power) implies a political ideology, political organization and a revolutionary goal. Real guerrilla warfare may be seen as a combination of military violence and of political power.

The evolution away from violence

Violence arising out of popular frustration and anger may therefore be seen either as a pre-political phenomenon, or as the culmination of a political movement. In the evolution of the suffrage and labour movements in Britain, riots and sabotage largely pre-dated more highly organized and articulate movements of artisans and labourers. The riots that did occur in the eighteenth century also evolved towards a greater political awareness. The movement in support of Wilkes indicated this new level of awareness, though sporadic violence accompanied both the industrial and political elements in the popular disturbances of this time.

George Rudé draws on contemporary accounts to describe some of these incidents. During the coal heavers' strike, for example, the house of a publican instrumental in trying to break the strike 'was beseiged by angry coal-heavers, armed with cutlasses and bludgeons, who demolished his windows and a panel of his front door, but were repulsed by musket-fire' (*Wilkes and Liberty*, 97). At the height of the confrontation between the City of London and parliament over the printing of parliamentary debates, parliament was surrounded by crowds of up to 50,000 people, who impeded MPs trying to enter the House, and Lord North's carriage was broken up by the crowd whilst he narrowly escaped with his life.

Rudé concludes that Wilkes's achievement was 'to harness the political energies and support of many thousands . . . who had previously been considered outside the "political nation" and had remained untouched by parliamentary or municipal elections' (ibid., 196). Rudé comments on the nature of the mass demonstrations and riots associated with Wilkes that they were quite different from the mobs manufactured to promote the interests of an individual politician. The crowds demonstrating for Wilkes did so 'in a cause which they believed, however vaguely and incoherently, to be their own' (ibid., 197). Rudé adds that the element of political consciousness raised the movement 'above the level of a mere food riot or such blind outbursts as those provoked by the employment of Irish labour and the passage of the Gin Act of 1736' (ibid.).

The evolution from rioting towards organized political protest marked not only a new consciousness and self-discipline but a greater possibility of effectiveness. Edward Thompson reports that when thousands of well-drilled spinners marched through Manchester, whilst out on strike in 1818, a general who was watching commented that: 'The peaceable demeanour of so many thousand unemployed Men is not natural.' Thompson adds: 'It is a phrase worth pausing over. The gentry, who had decried the reformers as a rabble, were appalled and some were even panic-stricken when they found that they were *not*' (*The Making of the English Working Class*, 681).

By the time of the Chartist movement the violence which was threatened was not that of sporadic rioting but of organized and armed insurrection. This threat was dramatized by Chartists who attended mass meetings armed, and summed up in their slogan: 'peaceably if we may, forcibly if we must'. Dorothy Thompson, when analysing the actual role of violence in the Chartist movement, concludes:

> Given that Chartism was a popular movement, rooted in the communities of the working people, an interesting phenomenon is the rarity of what might be called 'folk violence'. The manifestations of violent protest which were most common in villages and townships—the pillorying of unpopular individuals by effigy-burning or rough music, sporadic outbreaks of arson, machine-breaking or cattle-houghing directed against unpopular employers or magistrates, were almost unknown amongst the Chartists. Although such occurrences were probably becoming rarer in the nineteenth century, they certainly occurred in this period in the agricultural districts, and recur again in popular demonstrations against the Cobdenite Liberals during the Crimean War and the 'pro-Boers' in the Boer War (*The Early Chartists*, 16–17).

The extension of the franchise and of forms of constitutional protest has naturally tended to limit the occasions on which mass resistance or rebellion appears appropriate. Moreover, the development of an organized labour movement has tended to replace the threat of armed insurrection with the threat of mass non-co-operation through a general strike. It was industrial action, not armed resistance, which the labour movement threatened in 1919 to prevent war with the Soviet Union. Where constitutional government is threatened by a military *coup d'état* the classic response is a general strike, like that undertaken against the Kapp Putsch in 1919, and planned by the French trade unions in the face of a potential *coup* by Algerian paratroopers in 1961.

Even where the aim is insurrection rather than resistance the primary emphasis in both Marxist and syndicalist thought has not been on military skill, but on the organization and political consciousness of the working class. The general strike was seen by the syndicalists as a possible prelude to insurrection, to be supplemented by mutiny in the armed forces. Marxist theory recognized the probable necessity of using military force to combat counter-revolutionary groups. But Marxists analysing the February and October Revolutions have tended to stress the importance of political, not military, action by workers and soldiers. Isaac Deutscher claimed in the course of discussion on violence and non-violence that:

> The October insurrection was carried out in such a way that, according to all the hostile eyewitnesses such as the Western ambassadors who were then in Petrograd, the total number of victims on all sides was ten. . . . The revolution was won not with guns, but with words, with argument, persuasion (*Liberation*, July 1969, 13).

The role of riots

It is strange, in view of the pre-political nature of much popular violence, that riots should be seen now as proof of the political effectiveness of 'violence'. Since the riots in American cities during the 1960s are cited as evidence for this view, it is worth considering both the political content of these riots, and their results. Although the riots had political overtones and implications—they were often sparked off by police brutality—most were not specifically political in origin. (An obvious exception was the wave of rioting which followed the death of Martin Luther King.) Neither were they a direct attack on white society. Kenneth B. Clark comments: 'It was the Negro ghetto in Los Angeles which Negroes looted and burned, not the white community. When white firemen tried to enter the ghetto, they were barred by Negro snipers' (in Endleman (ed.), *Violence in the Streets*, 288). He also notes that thirty-three of the thirty-six people killed were black.

Despite the fact that the political motivation was generalized and often indirect, there is no doubt that the riots had some political effect. They alarmed public opinion, worried the government, and led to the allocation of poverty funds. The effect of the riots was similar to that created by demonstrations like those in Birmingham. They created a challenge to public order and to the authority of the federal government. The credibility of governments depends on their ability to maintain order, and to remedy situations which create *justifiable* cause for unrest in the view of the press and of sections of the public. However, the method of rioting is less likely to appear a response to justifiable grievances than is peaceful civil disobedience. It is therefore arguable that the impact of the riots depended on the broader political context—Supreme Court and Congressional endorsement of the unconstitutional nature of discrimination, years of civil rights agitation, and a growing awareness not only of racialism, but of areas of poverty within the affluence of American society. It was belief in the legitimacy of the grievances behind the riots that promoted the response of trying to alleviate the poverty of the ghettos.

The other possible response, which was also manifested, was to redouble efforts to maintain 'law and order'. The shock effect of the rioting evoked both reactions—but it evoked a positive (though quite inadequate) response primarily because it could appeal to sympathy and guilt. Rioting undoubtedly evoked this response much more rapidly than orthodox political lobbying could have done—but if 'success' is to be understood in terms of gaining reforms or concessions, then rioting is liable in the long-run to jeopardize the conditions making for reform.

Substituting violence for power

One advantage of violence demonstrated by the ghetto riots was the amount of publicity and public attention they attained. Since publicity tends to be one of the main criteria for the impact and success of a protest, it is understandable that demonstrators should see advantages in deliberately staging 'a riot', or in the destruction of property. Nevertheless, at a tactical level even minor acts of violence have a tendency to alienate fringe sympathizers and the uncommitted. The *Guardian* account of the Madison students' activities against the Indo-China war (quoted at the end of chapter 3) reported:

> About 400 are working hard and constructively to end the war. Their projects include canvassing squads which go out daily into the suburbs to mobilise opinion against the war; . . . a committee which has been handing out a different leaflet every day outside the city's 14 factories and main office block; and a speakers' panel ready to talk to any organisation on the war.
> This latter committee is perhaps the best organised. . . . They admit that the trashing is turning away more and more of the workers they are trying to woo, and that there is now probably more anger among the workers against the student trashing than there is against

the war. But, like other Left-wing groups on the campus the committee's members refuse to condemn the violence (14 May 1970, 2).

The attractions and drawbacks of serious sabotage or assassination attempts are those of minor violence correspondingly magnified. Bomb explosions in the Pentagon or the London Post Office Tower are primarily forms of symbolic demonstration and advertisements for the cause, designed to make a point more dramatically and more 'forcefully' than a peaceful demonstration. Moreover, the violence of a bomb explosion is, in a sense, a substitute for the power of numbers. But physical destruction shocks not only in the sense of seizing attention, but in the sense of creating horror and revulsion. This is even more true if people are either accidentally or deliberately killed. As a form of demonstration 'propaganda by deed' lacks the public participation and the public expression of anger involved in either 'riots' or violent protests in the streets. And the advance calculation involved makes the resultant damage less forgivable.

The original acts of 'propaganda by deed' were carried out by some disillusioned Russian populists at the end of the last century, and by a small minority within the anarchist movement. Guérin observes that: 'The defection of the mass of the working class had been one of the reasons for the recourse to terrorism.' These methods were repudiated by Marxists as being irrelevant to the real task of organizing the workers. Syndicalists differed about the effect of this kind of 'propaganda'. Guérin quotes a veteran syndicalist who argued: 'It was like the stroke of a gong bringing the French proletariat to its feet after the prostration into which it had been plunged by the massacres of the Commune [and was] the prelude to . . . the mass trade-union movement of the years 1900–1910 (*Anarchism*, 75). But Pelloutier, one of the leaders of revolutionary syndicalism, 'believed the use of dynamite had deterred the workers from professing libertarian socialism, however disillusioned they might have been with parliamentary socialism' (ibid.).

The adoption of arson and bombing as a strategy of protest has in both America and West Germany been the conscious result of despairing of previous methods of resistance, and in particular, of action by the organized workers. It also stems from a sense of desperate urgency to alter conditions of poverty and injustice at home, and specifically to stop the Vietnam war. Violence promises a short-cut to effectiveness, and it may seem justified by the spectacle of much greater government violence. It provides too at a personal level a degree of commitment and danger which seem appropriate to a serious revolutionary goal. Because resort to warfare against the government, or society at large, is totally uncompromising it seems more revolutionary than forms of action which can be met by appropriate reforms—though the fact that no limited gains are possible greatly increases the likelihood of total defeat. Neither is any form of 'victory' possible so long as violence is merely a form of minority demonstration.

Guerrilla tactics

The main reason why bomb explosions, arson and shooting at policemen have been adopted by groups like the Weathermen is that they are seen as the first stage of a genuine guerrilla campaign. The difficulty with this view is that white left-wing radicals have no natural base in the United States from which to launch guerrilla warfare. Tom Hayden comments that the Weathermen were more like commandos operating behind the enemy lines, and that they tended as a result to see as enemies the vast majority of the American people. Members of the Baader-Meinhof group actually received guerrilla training from Arab guerrillas, but they were even more isolated in West German society than the Weathermen in America.

The most serious political result of small-scale attempts to practise guerrilla tactics is that the authorities may react by curbing civil liberties and suppressing all forms of unorthodox opposition. Bombings and shootings are likely to be seized upon by the Right as a means of discrediting the Left. The exaggerated publicity given by the Springer Press to the Baader-Meinhof 'gang' illustrates this point. Moreover, the threat of left-wing violence has often been used by fascist groups anxious to introduce their own version of 'law and order'. To dramatize the threat of violence, where the power to consolidate a revolutionary movement does not exist, is to maximize the opportunities of authoritarian or fascist groups. In addition when the Left adopts or advocates tactics identical to those of the far Right they blur the political and moral distinction between their ultimate goals. They also lay themselves open to being made responsible for terrorist action by their opponents. The fact that four Italian anarchists were held in prison for three years awaiting trial for a bomb explosion in a Milan bank which killed sixteen people, and that two neo-fascists were formally charged in connection with the same explosion thirty-three months later, illustrates the reality of this danger.

The only circumstances in which a strategy of guerrilla warfare seems feasible in western society is where there is a clearly defined community, suffering enough injustice and discrimination to be predisposed to back those who wage war on the wider society. The support for the Provisional IRA in the Catholic ghettos of Ulster is an obvious example—though the Northern Ireland situation had, from the IRA standpoint, elements of a classic nationalist and anti-colonialist campaign. The black ghettos in the American cities are in the view of a number of Black Power spokesmen a natural base for urban guerrilla warfare. Indeed, one of the long-term threats posed by the riots was that they might be harnessed to a strategy of guerrilla fighting. Tom Hayden suggested in *Rebellion in Newark* that:

> Men are now appearing in the ghettos who might turn the energy of the riot in a more organized and continuous revolutionary direction. . . . During a riot, for instance, a conscious guerrilla can participate in pulling police away from the path of people engaged in attacking stores (in Oppenheimer, *Urban Guerrilla*, 32).

However, this threat of guerrilla organization in the ghettos, which was like much of the Black Power rhetoric intended largely as a form of blackmail, did not materialize.

The problems of 'self-defence'

The organization which was active in the late 1960s was the Black Panthers, who rejected a strategy of armed assault on white society, but did espouse very publicly a strategy of self-defence against the police. Although the Panther leadership stressed the defensive nature of their guns, the high 'visibility' of their guns and uniforms could be interpreted as a provocation. Moreover, the rhetorical emphasis given to 'self-defence' encouraged a tendency to switch to the offensive in using the gun. A contributor to *Village Voice* described a Black Panther meeting in September 1970, and recorded that a speaker 'gave a loving description of the Panther version of self-defense':

> 'It means if the pig moves on you today and he's got a gun, and, you ain't got a gun, Christ, hippie, you ain't in a position to deal with him'; he said, adding after a pause 'but come sundown. . . .' The crowd in the gym . . . broke into happy laughter, cheering and applause. . . . 'You go up on the roof . . .' (Another pause and more cheers), 'You put your finger on that index' (Cheers again) 'You get him in your sights' (Cheers) 'And you pull that trigger . . .' (Wild cheers). 'That's self-defense. Cause if you don't get him today, he's gonna get you tomorrow' (*Liberation*, Autumn 1970, 72–3).

By 1971 Panther leader Huey Newton had come to the conclusion that in trying to fight the police all they had achieved was 'a lot of bloodshed'. After splitting with the exiled Eldridge Cleaver, Newton declared that the Panthers would abandon violence. He also felt that the Panthers had made a political error. Newton said in San Francisco in May 1971: 'We thought of ourselves as a vanguard. . . . However, when we looked around we found we were not the vanguard for anything . . . we lost the favor of the Black community and left it behind. . . . We cannot jump from A to Z as some thought' (*Keesings*, 22–9 April 1972, 25218). A year later on 5 June

1972 Newton told a *Guardian* reporter: 'We have rejected the rhetoric of the gun. . . . Our goal now is to organise the black communities politically' (4).

The image of the gun caused another difficulty which the Panthers recognized much earlier. Bobby Seale comments that: 'The Black Panther Party has had problems with a lot of people who come in and use the Party as a base for criminal activity which the Party never endorsed.' This complication might arise for any movement recruiting in the ghetto. But, as Seale records: 'Some brothers would come into the Party, and see us with guns, and they related *only* to the gun.' He also observes:

> Some people joined the Party for status reasons. . . . These cats would put on a complete Panther uniform. . . . They were psychologically surviving off the incorrect sensationalism that had been put forth in the newspapers. We began to call them the 'do-nothing terrorists' (*Seize the Time*, 405–7).

The Panthers had the advantages of representing a community which was generally acknowledged to be suffering injustice, of being able to claim genuine support in that community, and of employing a form of 'violence' sanctioned by the American ethos. Nevertheless, they suffered disastrous losses at the hands of the police—and although any militant black grouping is liable to arouse police hostility, the 'rhetoric of the gun' increased the likelihood of police violence. According to Newton, they lost their support; and on Seale's evidence the glamour of violence tended to distract members from political activity, and to mislead the public about their real aims. The experience of the Panthers can therefore be seen as an illustration of the general dangers of a strategy involving violence.

The advantages of non-violent tactics can be deduced directly from the drawbacks of violence. When violence is clearly directed *against* demonstrators—as at Sharpeville or Birmingham, then it tends to promote sympathy for their cause and revulsion against the authorities. Fanon comments:

> The murders of Sharpeville shook public opinion for months. In the newspapers, over the wavelengths and in private conversations Sharpeville has become a symbol. It was through Sharpeville that men and women first became acquainted with the problem of apartheid in South Africa (*The Wretched of the Earth*, 59).

But he does not point out that the impact of the Sharpeville shootings lay largely in the fact that the crowd was unarmed, as the impact of police brutality in Birmingham was underlined by the peaceful behaviour of the demonstrators.

The disadvantages of non-violence

Generalizations about 'non-violence' can however be misleading if different styles of non-violence, and the appropriateness of modes of protest to the ends to be achieved, is ignored. The reasons for adopting non-violence can stem from weakness and an accompanying prudence; from a desire to prove respectability and win liberal sympathy; from a concern to tone down the militance of direct action in order to placate public opinion, or because of unease about the legitimacy of disturbing public order; or from a committed belief in the moral value and superiority of non-violence and the special quality it gives to the movement. Inge Powell Bell in her study of *CORE and the Strategy of Nonviolence* suggests all these elements were present in the early civil rights struggles and in the speeches of Martin Luther King.

The argument from weakness is politically convincing, but in practice it may create strategic and psychological problems. One of the main values of a direct action movement in its early stages is its effect on those taking part—creating a sense of purpose, pride and self-confidence and a belief that change is possible. It is not easily compatible with this dawning assertiveness and newly demonstrated courage to emphasize the reality of political weakness. Moreover, excessive concern about one's weakness may undermine a strategy of direct action, which invites hostility, often means breaking the law, and always incurs criticism from orthodox supporters.

Awareness of weakness will also discourage progress to more militant forms of direct action; Miss Bell records the attempts by liberals sympathetic to the initial sit-ins to end the freedom rides, which they regarded as more inflammatory. Those who undertake direct action may try to combine calculated risks with reasonable prudence, but the meaning of prudence in this context is not clearly defined. An agreed compromise is always liable to be interpreted as a cowardly withdrawal, or as a sell-out by the leadership.

Both the desire to prove respectability and the related anxiety to justify one's militancy may be natural to movements of those previously conditioned to feel inferior. The early Suffragettes, unlike many of today's Women's Liberation activists, were anxious to emphasize their femininity even whilst claiming equality and indulging in aggressive forms of protest. Christabel Pankhurst comments:

> It was always interesting to note the revulsion of feeling, and to
> hear the change of tone of the critics who had gained their
> opinion of the conflict at second-hand, when they discovered that
> the Suffragettes were not fanatics and viragos but just ordinary
> women who had made up their minds to get political fair play.
> Mother, especially, made converts in thousands, even before she

had begun her speech, simply by her appearance and manner, which were so completely different from all expectation (*Unshackled*, 60).

The Southern black students taking part in the sit-ins were at pains to emphasize their good manners. Their demeanour had immediate advantages. Zinn quotes the editorial comment in the Virginian *Richmond News Leader* in February 1960:

> Many a Virginian must have felt a tinge of wry regret at the state of things as they are, in reading of Saturday's 'sit-downs' by Negro students in Richmond stores. Here were the colored students in coats, white shirts, ties, and one of them was reading Goethe and one was taking notes from a biology text. And here, on the sidewalk outside, was a gang of white boys come to heckle, a ragtail rabble, slack-jawed, black-jacketed, grinning fit to kill, and some of them, God save the mark, were waving the proud and honored flag of the Southern States in the last war fought by gentlemen. Eheu! It gives one pause (*SNCC : The New Abolitionists*, 27).

It is doubtful, however, if this desire to conform to social convention stems primarily from a sense of inferiority. Peace movements have often been at pains to persuade demonstrators to cut their hair and look as conventional as possible in order to avoid giving irrelevant offence. Any movement taking the plunge into a largely hostile society and concerned to influence public opinion feels the need to justify itself and refute hostile stereotypes. Neither does awareness that some methods of protest are controversial necessarily indicate doubts about the justice of one's cause. But it is reasonable that groups who are demanding their basic rights should be more self-confident and more impatient than a minority trying to persuade the majority to change national policy on, for example, defence.

Attitudes to methods are also linked to the nature of one's goals. When the civil rights campaign for integration was replaced by Black Power calling for a mixture of 'nationalist' independence and socialism, the former non-violent style was rejected not only for its association with weakness, but for its kowtowing to liberal opinion and reformist middle-class philosophy. The Uncle Tom elements in non-violence were exaggerated by Black Power militants—but some evidence for their view can be found in the approach and rhetoric of Martin Luther King. A contributor to *Liberation* remarked that: 'Part of the confusion about non-violence is rooted in the person and image of Martin Luther King' (January 1967, 20).* But Miss Bell suggests that non-violence was

---

* The author of the article, Lon Clay Hill, criticizes King for attempting to mediate between the mayors and rioters of New York, Chicago and Los Angeles, and for being 'so anxious to prevent *Negroes* from being violent that he has supported the

rejected above all because it failed to give vent to the suppressed anger of the rank and file who took part in direct action, and was felt to imply an apology for militance and therefore an admission of inequality—a sense that equality had to be 'earned', not demanded as a right.

She argues all these disadvantages might have been overcome if non-violence could have established itself as the *best* philosophy and mode of action. But although non-violence did in the early stages have the function of promoting a sense of moral superiority and of a mission to redeem white society, it had no real cultural or social underpinning in American society. Abstract moral superiority tended to give way to a more personal and physical sense of pride.

On the other hand, it is arguable that non-violence lost ground so quickly precisely because it claimed to be an overall philosophy, and because it developed its own rhetoric which tended to be sentimental, and overstressed moral and emotional appeal. For example, W. Haywood Burns noted:

> The buying power of the Negro community represents a crucial factor in the economic system of most Southern areas. . . . The campaigns in Nashville, Tennessee and Tuskegee, Alabama are prime examples of the many campaigns of economic withdrawal by Negroes which have been eminently successful. 'Economic withdrawal' rather than 'boycott' is the term preferred by many in the movement. They point out that theirs is a moral crusade and as such should use moral means to achieve its ends (*The Voices of Negro Protest in America*, 49).

A reaction against sentiment and moralism therefore looked like a greater realism. The tendency of spokesmen for non-violent action to underplay the economic and political coercion involved, encouraged the view that coercion was the only important factor, and that what was required was a more potent form of coercion—violence. The appeal of non-violence as an ideal was particularly vulnerable to a change in style and tone.

Non-violence as a total philosophy is also vulnerable because it implies a pacifist commitment which has so far always been limited to a small minority. It also draws such a sharp dividing line between non-violence and 'violence' that it tends to blur distinctions between types and levels of violence. It is only against an advocacy of exclusive non-violence that the issue of self-defence could have become a subject for heated ideological debate; and that the 'victory' of self-defence, among those for whom it

use of the National Guard to restore "law and order". . . . It would be better to remain silent than be in a position so much like supporting King George after the Boston Tea Party'.

was a largely abstract issue, could have signalled a total defeat for a strategy of non-violence when allied to direct action. As James Farmer suggests, the major failure of non-violence was to prove itself as a political tactic, one which could be adopted by people of varied political commitments:

> Were nonviolence offered strictly as a tactic, a method which is effective in achieving certain limited results under various specific circumstances, then the guntoters might be persuaded to leave the hardware at home. . . . If the tactic is shrouded in cosmic principle, however, its rejection as a way of life destroys it as a tactic too (in Goldwin (ed.), *On Civil Disobedience*, 133).

The image of passivity

Despite the model of non-violent direct action provided by the civil rights movement, many commentators make no clear distinction between this form of action and guerrilla tactics. Indeed, the style of reporting on protest demonstrations tend to blur the distinction. George Kennan comments: 'The world seems to be full, today, of embattled students. . . . Photographs of them may be seen daily: screaming, throwing stones, breaking windows, overturning cars, being beaten or dragged about by police' (*Democracy and the Student Left*, 7). The author of *Rebels in Eden*, Richard Rubenstein, states: 'More than five years of assassinations, ghetto uprisings, student revolts, tumultous demonstrations and violent police action have produced no systematic revaluation of the role of political violence in American history' (4).

Rebels in Eden identifies 'non-violence' with working through the conventional political processes—which is one frequent interpretation. Another common interpretation is to identify non-violence with pure passivity. For example, Truman Nelson, in his introduction to Robert Williams's argument for self-defence, rejected King's emphasis on the Gandhian concept of voluntary suffering in the following terms: 'Two hundred years of appeal by accumulative suffering to the hearts of racists is enough, enough, enough! The American Negro is not a downtrodden Hindu, a palpitating mass of ingrained and inborn submission to being put in his place' (*Nation*, 22 April 1968, 543). This passage ignores the distinction between suffering passively endured, and suffering incurred as the result of resistance. Herbert Marcuse argues that: 'Non-violence is normally not only preached to but exacted from the weak—it is a necessity rather than a virtue, and normally does not seriously harm the case of the strong.' He goes on to explain away apparent examples of successful non-violent action, like Gandhi's campaign in India:

> Passive resistance was carried through on a massive scale, which

disrupted, or threatened to disrupt, the economic life of the country. Quantity turns into quality: on such a scale, passive resistance is no longer passive—it ceases to be non-violent. The same holds true for the General Strike (in Wolff, *et al.*, *A Critique of Pure Tolerance*, 116).

Emphasis on the 'passivity' of non-violent action tends to imply by contrast that violence is *the* essential form of self-assertion and of action. In her study *On Violence* Hannah Arendt oscillates between a view of violence as symbolized by the bomb and the gun, and a quite different concept of violence as a desperate attempt to break through to political effectiveness. The 'violence' of current protest is primarily, in this interpretation, an attempt to recapture the creative power stemming from free co-operation and epitomized in the ideal of direct democracy. It would be more illuminating to see this latter conception of 'violence', which is identified particularly with the student movement, as an attempt to set in motion social power—as 'direct action'.

The role of government

The distinction between power and violence can be applied not only to protest movements but to the sphere of government. The power of government lies in the effective co-ordination of all sections of administration, but above all in the active co-operation of its citizens in running society and their willingness to observe the laws. Because the power of government depends on co-operation it can be eroded by non-co-operation. Conversely, a government which can rely on its power—and not on violence—is less likely to be faced with movements of serious protest.

Since all governments rely on some degree of physical coercion it is helpful to distinguish between what is normally accepted as legitimate force, and extreme or unnecessary brutality, or 'violence'. Some instances of police behaviour, like that in Chicago in 1968, have been widely recognized to depart from normal police methods of controlling demonstrations (though what is acceptable and normal varies between countries and even cities). The shooting of unarmed civilians, for example, by British paratroopers at Derry, is usually seen not as law enforcement, but as murder.

One result of violence by the police or army is that it evokes an overall image of 'violent' protest, even if the demonstrators have refrained from violence or resorted to it solely in self-defence. Excess violence by the authorities may also provoke a violent response from protesters, either as an immediate reaction or as a longer-term strategy. Tom Hayden writes about the Weathermen:

Many Weathermen leaders were shaped by the events of Chicago 1968. When our legal protest was clubbed down, they became

outlaws. When our pitiful attempts at peaceful confrontation
were overwhelmed, they adopted the tactic of offensive guerrilla
violence. When our protest against the war failed, they decided to
bring the war home (*Trial*, 92).

If the authorities, by allowing police to run riot, or by deliberately
planning brutal suppression (on the evidence a more plausible interpretation of police behaviour in Chicago), can create violence by dissenters,
they can also encourage violence by using inadequate force to uphold the
law. Failure to apply the law strictly may be due to inherent government
weakness, but more often is due to the bias and selectivity in the use of
government force. The Weimar government allowed brown shirt gangs to
terrorize Jews and beat up their left-wing opponents, but the courts and
police were much less lenient towards the Left. The United States
federal government has sanctioned defiance of the law and illegal violence
by Southern state governments and police. Howard Zinn in his study of
the SNCC, a study which favours non-violent tactics, comments that:

> There is one powerful justification for asking Negroes in the Deep
> South to stick to nonviolence in the face of the terrible measures
> used against them by private and official forces in the Black Belt;
> that is, that they live in a nation where the power of the federal
> government can disarm and neutralize those who would take away
> their constitutional liberties. *But thus far the federal government has
> not done this* (*SNCC: The New Abolitionists*, 213–14).

On the other hand, the federal government gave evidence of being
willing to prosecute civil rights demonstrators. As John Lewis said in
Washington in August 1963:

> In Albany, Georgia, nine of our leaders have been indicted not by
> Dixiecrats but by the Federal Government for peaceful protest.
> But what did the Federal Government do when Albany's Deputy
> Sheriff beat Attorney C. B. King and left him half-dead? What did
> the Federal Government do when local police officials kicked and
> assaulted the pregnant wife of Slater King, and she lost her baby?
> (in ibid., 211).

More recently police zeal in arresting members of the Black Panther
Party and in shooting others contrasts with the absence of police action
against right-wing groups sporting their own arsenals, like the Minutemen.

If the government gives the impression of being too brutal, too weak or
too partial in its application of the laws, then the legitimacy of government
force and the authority of the government will be questioned by sections
of the community who feel they are being attacked and discriminated
against, or are not receiving the protection of the law. A constitutionalist

critique of illegal or violent action by protest movements must also address itself therefore to the constitutionalism of the government's own actions.

5 Civil disobedience and constitutionalism

Direct action is often seen as a threat to liberal democracy. But liberal democratic theory comprises three separate strands: eighteenth-century constitutionalism as celebrated by Whig theory and the American constitution; liberalism which adds nineteenth-century conceptions of individualism, rationalism and tolerance; and democratic egalitarianism stemming from the French Revolution, but transmuted into parliamentary forms.

The constitutionalist heritage is itself a complex combination of tradition and of abstract theory. It has its roots in the legal and customary checks and balances of the Middle Ages, and is still symbolized by the law courts and by parliament. Superimposed on this institutional inheritance is the social contract theory of the seventeenth century, with its rationalist view of social obligation and its theory of natural rights, and its affirmation—in the version popularized by Locke—of the right of rebellion against tyranny. As the medieval division of powers gave way to the increasing power of the centralizing monarchy, seventeenth-century constitutionalism was justified partly on the basis of a more abstract theory, as well as on the ancient prerogatives of parliament. Because constitutionalism was finally asserted in both Britain and America by rebellion against excess executive power, a political theory which stressed the role of law had as its foundation myth a violent and glorious revolution. Hence, as noted in chapter 2, later movements could hark back to the idea of a legitimate uprising against tyranny; and in America this concept still has rhetorical validity.

But the predominant emphasis of constitutionalism is the need for political checks and balances and the overriding importance of respect for the laws: for the fundamental laws (or conventions) of the constitution and for the common law of the land, both of which should be the bulwark of the liberties of the individual citizen. The conception of liberty involved is one of 'negative' liberty—the absence of arbitrary governmental restraints and impositions on the individual. It is also one of concrete liberty or right, protected by custom, by the traditions of the constitution itself, and by prevailing sentiments. But as abstracted and generalized in the American Declaration of Independence, and then in the French revolutionary version of the Rights of Man, concrete liberties were given a basis in universalized principles of human rights, which could be taken up by groups excluded from the customary liberties and privileges of society. The natural law and natural rights basis of social contract theory also provide grounds for appeal by dissenters prepared to break the law or defy the constitution in the interests of a higher law, or more universal considerations of justice. But the social contract approach at the same time stresses the citizens' obligation to the society and government which provide him with many of the blessings which he enjoys, and both the social contract theory and the older constitutional tradition evoke the idea of duties parallel to rights—for example, the duty to fight for one's country.

Some forms of direct action, like strikes, have, as already indicated, won themselves constitutional status. But in general direct action means a direct or indirect threat to public order, involving disobedience to specific laws, or forms of physical intervention, likely to be construed as illegal. Many forms of direct action can therefore be designated under the general heading of 'civil disobedience'. In its strict interpretation civil disobedience suggests refusal to comply with a law which is in itself regarded as immoral, or an unjustifiable infringement of one's rights. Trade union non-co-operation with industrial legislation restricting trade union rights would fall into this category. But most recent examples of 'civil disobedience' in Britain and the United States have involved illegal action to protest against an evil or unjust policy or situation, rather than direct disobedience of a specifically unjust law.

The constitutional arguments for disobedience

In what circumstances can 'civil disobedience' be justified by constitutional theory? The most obvious case is where recognized constitutional rights are being abrogated by the government, or denied at a local level. Local denial of constitutional rights has often been the reason for protests in the civil rights struggle, though the precise legal position has varied. In the most clear-cut cases of all, a Supreme Court decision has been flouted by Southern states. This was the position when the 1961 freedom riders set out to test desegregation of facilities at bus terminals for interstate buses. More often, the protesters were asserting a right which they believed came within the spirit of the constitution and of the Supreme Court attitude to desegregation in its recent rulings—as when the sit-in demonstrators demanded the right to eat in desegregated restaurants, a right granted in the 1964 Civil Rights Act. Frequently also civil rights demonstrators faced local police bans on peaceful processions and the right of assembly, rights guaranteed under the First Amendment.

Because civil rights demonstrations could claim either the immediate blessing of constitutional legality, or after being fought through the courts could be proved to be legal, or could retrospectively claim authority from subsequent Congressional legislation, it is possible to argue that these demonstrations were not really forms of civil disobedience at all, but an assertion of legal rights.* However, the constitutionality of direct action

---

* See William L. Taylor, 'Civil disobedience: observations on the strategies of protest', in Bedau (ed.), *Civil Disobedience.*

is not always so easily settled. If the Supreme Court had ruled against a case involving peaceful assembly in defiance of local prohibition, or if Congress had failed to legislate in favour of integration of restaurants, the demonstrators would still maintain that their acts though formally illegal were in the spirit of the constitution. If direct action had occurred in the interwar years it would most probably not have had the backing of the Supreme Court, because it is only since 1954 that the Supreme Court has adopted a positive role in promoting civil rights, and earlier in the century it often gave constitutional sanction to Southern devices to evade granting voting or other rights to negroes. The attitude of the Supreme Court of course reflects a change in political mood, and the approach of both the Court and Congress in the 1960s were themselves influenced by the movement of direct action for civil rights. The specific legality of direct action is therefore primarily a matter of political, not technical, interpretation.

An appeal to constitutional rights is less a matter of strict legality than an appeal to the spirit of the constitution. This ambiguity is inherent in the very concept of constitutionalism, which implies general and abstract principles of justice and right that may or may not be present in a specific paper constitution; and which may often be present in the letter but totally ignored in practice. An appeal to the constitution—as in the case of Dolci's reverse strike in Sicily, when demonstrators appealed to the clause stating the duty of Italian citizens to work—is therefore always in part a rhetorical and political device. But its effectiveness is greatly enhanced where these rights do exist in legal theory, and where constitutional rights have often been recognized in fact in the past.

The gap between the constitutional ideal and the realities of politics means that it may often be possible to charge with some plausibility that a particular government policy or piece of legislation is unconstitutional. The Special Powers Act introduced in Ulster in the emergency of 1922, for instance, was made permanent in 1936. This meant according to a National Council for Civil Liberties statement at the time: 'That through the use of Special Powers individual liberty is no longer protected by law, but is at the arbitrary disposition of the Executive. This abrogation of the rule of law has been so practised as to bring the freedom of the subject into contempt' (*Peace Press*, October–November 1971, 3). But given the complexities of precedent surrounding both written and unwritten constitutions of any antiquity, interpreting what is 'constitutional' is frequently contentious.

Hence the advantage of asserting that particular policies, even if they do not infringe the laws and constitution of the state, do infringe the laws of international society which the state is committed to honour. This claim can be made with the greatest certainty where precise legislation, precedents and an appropriate international tribunal, like the Hague

Court, exist to which an individual defendant can appeal against his own or another government. For example, the European Human Rights Commission decided that a case of discrimination could be made against the British government in light of the 1968 Commonwealth Immigrants Act. The position is then analogous to the civil rights demonstrator appealing to the Supreme Court—though given the weakness of international community, it is not the same, either legally or politically.

The appeal to international law may be based on a more generalized enunciation of accepted principles. The Nuremberg principles have been cited in justification of their disobedience by American draft-resisters. But how far these principles can be stretched to justify draft-resistance or besieging the Pentagon is disputable. Telford Taylor, who was the US chief counsel at Nuremberg, argues that the Nuremberg trials convicted only the top leadership, and acquitted a number of men on the charge of waging aggressive war on the ground they were not privy to Hitler's plans (*Nuremberg and Vietnam*). Therefore although the Nuremberg trials did extend the principle that individuals might be required to disobey their own government, in order to comply with international law, they did not explicitly extend it to individuals co-operating at any level in the prosecution of a war. Charles Wyzanski claims that the Nuremberg principles are adequately fulfilled if the individual refuses to obey at the point he is directly ordered to participate in committing a crime. The Nuremberg Judgment recognized that:

> No one may properly be charged with a crime unless he personally participated in it by doing the wrong or by purposefully aiding, abetting, and furthering the wrong . . . merely to fight in an aggressive war is no crime. What is a crime is personally to fight by foul means (in Bedau (ed.), *Civil Disobedience*, 200).

The appeal to Nuremberg is a more concrete, and polemical, version of the fundamental appeal to the universal principles of natural law, which underlie both constitutionalism and international law. Natural law was conceived by Roman jurists as a standard of permanent right and wrong based on rational understanding of the precepts which should ideally govern human conduct, and should therefore inform the laws of particular nations and the codes of conduct between nations. Although neither the original conception nor its later modifications fit neatly into our contemporary world view, an implicit natural law theory lies behind the United Nations Charter and any attempt to adduce universal standards of justice. In practice, the difficulties of interpreting and applying natural law may be no greater now than they were for the Roman jurists whose attempts were not free from ambiguity or contradictions.

It is possible to attack not only the legality of the content of particular policies, but also the way in which they have been adopted. Campaigners for nuclear disarmament sometimes argued that since the Attlee government deliberately concealed from parliament the development of the atomic bomb, the origins of British nuclear strategy lay in an entirely arbitrary executive act, and the British bomb only received belatedly the formality of a parliamentary endorsement of defence estimates. Paul Goodman argued in a symposium on civil disobedience over Vietnam:

> We hold that it is the Vietnam Policy that is illegitimate. It has been created by a hidden government of military-industrial lobbyists and the C.I.A.; the Executive has gone beyond his mandate; there has been no genuine debate and voting in Congress; the public has been lied to and brain-washed. The Government is a usurper, so sovereignty reverts to the people more directly (ibid., 206).

The usurpation of power in the conduct of the Vietnam War may be seen as illustrative of a much wider usurpation, manifested particularly in the conduct of defence policy, where executive discretion is very wide and where military considerations are closely linked to economic interests in the armaments industry. Justice William O. Douglas extends this critique to federal agencies like the Forest Service, the Bureau of Land Management and the Bureau of Public Roads, who, he argues, exercise their discretion in favour of the cattle barons, the lumber companies and the highway lobby. Douglas concludes: 'We must realize that today's Establishment is the new George III. Whether it will continue to adhere to his tactics, we do not know. If it does, the redress, honored in tradition, is also revolution' (*Points of Rebellion*, 95).

Douglas represents a libertarian and rebellious strand in constitutionalist thinking, which extols liberty and active citizenship, and is prepared to justify rebellion against excessive and arbitrary power. But usually the constitutionalist frame of mind puts a very high premium on the rule of law. Minor infringements of rights, or bad government policies, are not in themselves adequate grounds for disobedience. Constitutionalism does not encourage an apathetic citizenry; on the contrary, it celebrates an active sense of political responsibility. But dissent should be based on the existing constitutional and political modes of behaviour. The authority of the law and the constitution replaces the authority of the individual ruler, and should therefore be sacred—since the only perceived alternatives are arbitrary power or anarchy. Since the late eighteenth century the overall emphasis of constitutionalist theory has been conservative—a warding off of more extreme liberal or democratic demands. Burke is one of the best known exponents of this brand of constitutionalism, which is afraid of losing the liberties gained in the past due to the impatience of radicals in the present, deplores the quest for abstract perfection, and stresses the requirements of statesmanship: the need for realism, patience and compromise.

The case against civil disobedience

It is in this mood that George Kennan attacks student protesters: 'Human justice is always imperfect' he argues, and only qualified benefits can be expected from efforts to secure greater justice. 'But the good order of society is something tangible and solid. . . . The benefit of the doubt should lie, therefore, with the forces of order, not with the world-improvers' (*Democracy and the Student Left*, 170–1). It is also in this mood that a number of lawyers writing about civil disobedience frame their criticisms. The tone is caught in an article by Louis Waldman in the New York *State Bar Journal*, criticizing Martin Luther King:

> Correction of injustices by intimidation, by extra-legal means or inspired by fear of violence cannot longer be continued. And law enforcement authorities must make it clear that we are a constitutional government and the laws enacted pursuant to our Constitution must be obeyed whether the individuals or groups affected by these laws believe they are just or not. In absolute as well as relative terms, we in the United States have built a democratic constitutional system second to none. . . . It establishes the rule of law through constitutions and the Bill of Rights. Our nation has survived because of the dedication to these principles (in Bedau (ed.), *Civil Disobedience*, 114–15).

Waldman is representative of a school of thought which totally condemns civil disobedience, because obedience to the law is a social obligation, and disobedience will—it is argued—have a series of disastrous results. It will encourage general lawlessness; it will specifically encourage imitation by the most bitter opponents of the protesters; it will promote not only disorder but actual political violence; and it poses a fundamental threat to the constitution and to the parliamentary system.

The primary argument, that there is a social obligation to obey the laws of one's country, is not intended to be a universal generalization. If the basis of this obligation is an element of the social contract, then it may also be allowed that there is a right to disobedience if the government ceases to honour its part of this contract. Under Locke's interpretation disobedience is justified either if power is usurped unconstitutionally, or if power once lawfully gained is unlawfully used. Both Kennan and Waldman accept that under a fascist government disobedience might be admirable. It is only in a constitutional, or parliamentary, democracy that the law should be unconditionally obeyed. This is because government as well as subjects are constrained by the rule of law, and citizens have established channels of political influence and means of dissent. Kennan elaborates this point: 'The dimensions of this problem are not quite the same where the citizen has a part in determining public policy—where the social contract may be said to prevail—as they are where the feelings of the citizen are in no wise consulted in determining the policies of the state' (*Democracy and the Student Left*, 166–7).

The advocate of civil disobedience is often prepared to take up a more universal stance, and argue that at times men have an absolute obligation to disobey the laws of their state in the interests of a higher law. But this assertion does not tell us how we know what the higher law is or when it commands disobedience. As Martin Buber comments: 'Every attempt to answer this question on a general level in terms of unassailable validity must be doomed to failure' (in Urquhart (ed.), *A Matter of Life*, 51). The specific justification normally rests on an appeal to universal principle, combined with some reference to the misuse of government power in relation to a particular policy, or the abrogation of civil liberties, or to effective disenfranchisement. On the two latter counts a strong case could be made for civil disobedience by negroes in the South, deprived of the normal liberty to dissent and in most cases in the early 1960s, disenfranchized—indeed, in many ways the situation in the South fell outside the ambit of constitutional democracy. Waldman, however, refuses to accept Martin Luther King's claim that lack of the vote is sufficient grounds for disobedience—arguing that this would give children and aliens the same claim to flout the law. (Since minors and aliens have a recognized distinct status in law and in politics the comparison is not valid. The only group then who might reasonably claim disenfranchisement were draft-age men and women under the age of twenty-one who have now been given the vote.) But Waldman's main concern is not with the rights of disobedience, but with the danger to public order if the example is followed.

Indeed, the whole weight of the constitutionalist critique of illegal political action rests on the disruptive consequences of breaking the law, as any act of defiance is seen as promoting a general disregard for legality. Charles Wyzanski, for instance, argues that the protester who disobeys one law for the highest motives will then be more generally disposed to break the law. This proposition is over-simple. If the person in question is motivated by high-minded conscientious objection it is more likely that this frame of mind promotes continuing conscientious honesty. If conscientious civil disobedience is extended to a policy of resistance (a distinction explored later in this chapter) there may be a willingness to break rules or laws for political reasons, for example, smuggling deserters across frontiers, but this does not necessarily mean disregarding the law in general.

Wyzanski also comments that the individual who commits civil disobedience 'sets an example for others who may not have his pure motives. He weakens the fabric of society' (in Bedau (ed.), *Civil Disobedience*, 196). It is, however, implausible that acts of deliberate political disobedience have any effect on the general tendency to rob banks, forge banknotes, commit petty larceny, or become drunk and disorderly.

The actions of conscientious protesters enrolling in the campaigns of Martin Luther King, Bertrand Russell or Benjamin Spock are unlikely to have had much impact on the motives and values of either the criminal underworld or the poorer communities. Moreover, the sort of laws involved in civil disobedience are unlikely to be of the kind closely touching levels of general public legality. The reason why the widespread evasion of laws concerning drink, drugs or gambling can encourage general illegality is that many people want to indulge in these pursuits, because these fields offer opportunities for organized gangsters, and because the police are particularly open to bribery and participation in crime syndicates in these areas.*

It is also difficult to see why a campaign of civil disobedience would increase the incidence of petty lawbreaking by respectable citizens, for example, fiddling their income tax or breaking traffic rules. In fact this kind of middle-class illegal action illustrates the fallacy of assuming that breaking one type of law automatically leads to general lawlessness. The aura of respect and sanctity surrounding 'the law' may be held to exclude regulations concerning tax or traffic, when personal interest encourages infringement, and when social stigma does not attach to evasion.

The manner of civil disobedience is relevant too. Clearly protest which involves resort to bank robberies, shooting policemen and inciting ghetto riots does encourage a breakdown of public order. But there is a great gulf between this kind of guerrilla-style activity and civil disobedience, which usually means a peaceable, orderly and 'civil' breach of an unjust law; or a protest against unjust policies involving the breach of some law. The movements of civil disobedience in the civil rights campaign, in the nuclear disarmament movement, and in draft-resistance have usually complied with the Gandhian precepts for disobedience: openness in breaking the law and willingness to suffer the consequences. In addition, the protesters usually take pains to explain and justify this extraordinary step. It can therefore be claimed, as it was by Gandhi, that someone engaged in open civil disobedience is asserting his general respect for the law, and demonstrates this respect by his willingness to accept the penalty instead of trying to evade it. Harris Wofford paraphrasing Gandhi

---

* Nevertheless, W. H. Auden, in a reply to Kennan (printed in *Democracy and the Student Left*), justifies disobedience of these laws, classifying them as negatively unjust laws that the citizen has a right to disobey. He gives as an example the Prohibition Law, and argues that since a man has as much right to drink whisky as his neighbour has to drink milk, he also has a right privately to breach the law prohibiting alcohol. Since he is protecting his personal freedom of choice and his privacy he is under no obligation to the state to publicize or justify his disobedience.

However, where laws are positively unjust and command some kind of action, like enrolling in the army, it may be a civic duty to disobey these laws and to encourage others to follow suit.

writes: 'we are saying that we so respect the law that when we think it is so unjust that in conscience we cannot obey, then we belong in jail until that law is changed' (in ibid., 66).

George Kennan in his original *New York Times* article on student protest dismissed this argument, claiming that it provides no justification for breaking the law. Which is, in itself, true. But as a number of his correspondents pointed out, willingness to accept the consequences has never been the *primary* reason for breaking the law. It is, however, a relevant supplementary answer to the charge of fostering general lawlessness. Kennan also argued that open disobedience makes lawbreaking the privilege of the affluent. This comment occurs in the context of a rhetorical passage beginning: 'The violation of law is not, in the moral and philosophic sense, a privilege that lies offered for sale with a given price tag, like an object in a supermarket, available to anyone who has the price and is willing to pay for it' (*Democracy and the Student Left*, 18). If the price tag is two years in jail, true of many draft-resisters, or a beating-up in a southern jail—true for many civil rights demonstrators, then the advantages of affluence are not very obvious. And even when fines have been imposed it has quite often been the policy in civil disobedience campaigns to refuse to pay them. In fact though he does not revert specifically to the question of accepting the penalties of law breaking, Kennan slightly modifies his position in his reply to critics of his original article, and grants that there might be some occasions even in a parliamentary democracy, when individual conscience demands non-compliance with laws invading personal dignity.

Louis Waldman makes a particularly strong attack on the claim that open disobedience is better than secret illegality: 'The secret violator of law recognizes his act for what it is: an antisocial act; he may even be ashamed of what he is doing and seek to avoid disapprobation of his neighbours' (in Bedau (ed.), *Civil Disobedience*, 109). He may; but the main point of breaking the law secretly is to get away with it. Neither does secrecy necessarily prevent the lawbreaker from inciting and organizing others also to break the law. Waldman makes a more substantial point when he claims that 'the open violation of law is an open invitation to others to join in such violation'. If we dismiss the argument that this leads to more criminal disobedience, it is certainly possible that it may lead to more *political* disobedience, either in aid of the cause of the initial disobedience, or in aid of others. Waldman also points to the large numbers of groups with justifiable social or economic grievances, and concludes that widespread disobedience would lead to a total breakdown of public order.

There are several possible answers to this point. One is Locke's contention, in his justification of rebellion, that since political activism is unnatural to most people most of the time, they will only be stirred to revolt if provoked by major injustice and hardship. Where serious penalties may result from disobedience, resort to it requires considerable anger or conviction. The likelihood of imitation is greater among groups predisposed to political activism and facing less severe penalties as the prevalence of student unrest in the late 1960s suggested. But this also suggests a second point—that the widespread practice of essentially non-violent methods of direct action and disobedience—even if they are not based on the scrupulous requirements of Gandhian non-violence—does not necessarily lead to a breakdown of public order on any significant scale. Increased popular use of direct action by housewives worried about traffic, by homeless families, or men demanding the right to work, tends rather to reduce the degree of personal risk and social dislocation among sectors of society. There is therefore a case to be made that individual disobedience is necessary not only to promote governmental action to remedy injustice, but to assist the solution of problems which are being bypassed by an ineffective administration. If so, the fact that the example of disobedience inspires imitation is a reason for exemplifying the method.

It can, however, be argued that civil disobedience involves the greater danger of fostering violent forms of protest. Herbert Storing, for example, comments: 'I think it is now clear—as it should have been from the beginning—that the broad result of the propagation of civil disobedience is disobedience' (in Goldwin (ed.), *On Civil Disobedience*, 103–4). Storing argues that civil disobedience is an unsuccessful compromise between conventional political action and revolution. 'The fundamental choice lies, as Malcolm X often said, between bullets and ballots' (ibid., 96).

This line of argument does not show that illegal peaceful protest is in every case more likely to end in violence than a movement of constitutional protest which has become frustrated and which does not see a way forward through the ballot. Civil disobedience may radicalize the previously law-abiding, but it is also true that a conviction that the only real alternatives are either conventional pressure group tactics or armed revolt would lead any seriously disaffected group to reach for the gun—a position which tends to obtain now in certain countries. In the short-term, non-violent disobedience may channel the frustration of those who would otherwise turn to violence. Martin Luther King himself argued in his letter from Birmingham jail that given the factors promoting black militancy, for example, rapid decolonization in Africa, non-violent direct action was an alternative to 'ominous expressions of violence'.

In the longer-term, Storing is correct in suggesting that civil disobedience, and other forms of direct action, are an interim stage for a movement which seeks not minor reforms but basic social change. The discussion in chapter 3 suggested that a direct action movement might, depending both on the nature of the movement and the wider political context, turn either towards violence or towards political action. But it also suggested that the experience of direct action might result in a different style of political organization and activity. If this is true, then not only is civil disobedience and direct action an interim alternative to political lobbying or guerrilla tactics, but there is 'fundamentally' a third choice of political strategy.

Apart from fearing a general spread in lawlessness, and political imitation of tactics of civil disobedience, some critics have also stressed that disobedience incites the opponents of a movement adopting this method to follow suit. In relation to the civil rights campaign, this argument suggests that since the law has played a central role in promoting civil rights in the South, nothing should be done to encourage Southern defiance of the law. The examples of Southern non-co-operation and passive resistance in trying to maintain segregation—for example, by sending their children to all-white schools—seem to add weight to this contention. But the Southern states were mustering open defiance to the 1954 Supreme Court decision in favour of integration long before the civil rights campaign had become a major movement. Senator Harry Byrd of Virginia called for 'massive resistance' by the South early in 1956. Autherine Lucy was refused admission to the University of Alabama, after a riot by whites in 1956. Little Rock occurred in 1957. Deliberate slowness, not to say inaction, in implementing Supreme Court decisions was the reason for the freedom rides of 1961. Waldman argues that the Supreme Court has been responsible for the major advances in civil rights. But it was the mass civil rights demonstrations which forced the government to see that these decisions were implemented, and supplemented by further Congressional legislation.

The civil rights struggle on the whole presents the constitutional case for civil disobedience at its strongest. But there is no evidence that disobedience by peace protesters encourages their opponents to follow their example in openly defying the law. For one thing, their most influential opponents are in the government, or the armed forces, or in Congress, or in large corporations engaged in arms industry. Where extreme anti-Communist groups exist, like the John Birch Society and the Minutemen in the United States, they flourish by virtue of the cold war, McCarthyism, and of American political traditions favouring paranoid styles of politics. When they clash directly with anti-bomb or anti-Vietnam War movements they either organize legal counter-demonstrations, or engage in sabotage of peace offices, attacks on peace demonstrators and threats of assassination.

Both the civil rights and the anti-war movements have probably had some backlash effect, as manifested for instance in the Goldwater candidacy in 1964. But any active movement of dissent, even if strictly constitutional, would tend to provoke a reaction among opposing groups.

Indeed, Supreme Court decisions and Congressional Acts in favour of desegregation created a reaction in the South independent of civil rights protests—though the latter became a visible and obvious target for Southern hatred. The danger of a backlash is therefore a very tenuous reason for avoiding or abandoning a strategy of protest. There is in addition the inevitable uncertainty involved in trying to assess the political gains and losses from any action. Many commentators credit the 1963 campaign in Birmingham, Alabama, with being the catalyst which finally led President Kennedy to initiate extensive civil rights legislation. Certainly, the Birmingham demonstrations took place in April and May 1963. Kennedy proposed a new Civil Rights Act to Congress on 19 June. But many liberals in Birmingham, like the local clergy, deplored its effects on the city. It is also interesting that a committed civil rights attorney living in Birmingham, Charles Morgan, judged that the 1961 freedom rides resulted, through their timing, in defeating a moderate and energetic candidate for mayor of the city then in the midst of his campaign (see Morgan, *A Time to Speak*).

If the backlash is extensive, protest tactics may indirectly assist reactionary candidates seeking power—like Goldwater in 1964, or encourage factions already in power to bend the constitution in order to repress the dissidents. For example, Charles Wyzanski suggests that the Vietnam war-resisters could 'set the stage for a revival of a virulent McCarthyism, an administrative system of impressment into the armed forces, and the establishment of a despotic tyranny bent on impairing traditional civil liberties and civic rights' (in Bedau (ed.), *Civil Disobedience*, 197). If these dangers are real, however, it is very doubtful whether abstaining from active protest is the wisest strategy. Civil liberties are best eroded in an atmosphere of apathy and fear. McCarthyism flourished in the absence of any significant opposition. Consensus of respectable opinion, as indicated by the mass media and the public statements of politicians, may easily slide into a growing illiberalism. This has happened in Britain in relation to the increasingly restrictive legislation on immigration since 1963.

It may also be argued by critics of civil disobedience that even if the protest is non-violent it evokes a violent response. Waldman comments that 'the provocation of violence is violence'. Martin Luther King reacts angrily to accusations that black demonstrators were provoking counter-violence in Birmingham:

Isn't this like condemning the robbed man because his possession of money precipitated the evil act of robbery. . . . We must come to see that, as the federal courts have consistently affirmed, it is wrong to urge an individual to cease his efforts to gain his basic constitutional rights because the quest may precipitate violence.

Society must protect the robbed and punish the robber (*Why We Can't Wait*, 85–6).

The logic of Waldman's position leads to absurdity, since on these terms a Negro asserting his right to vote would be immorally provoking violence from a hostile sheriff.

Non-violent civil disobedience sometimes inevitably provokes counter-violence because of the very conditions which create the need for disobedience, and because it challenges the power and the privileges of one section of the community. This fact may lead to doubts about the political prudence of civil disobedience in some circumstances. Conor Cruise O'Brien predicted in October 1968, after the early successes of non-violent civil disobedience by the Civil Rights Movement in drawing British public attention to the injustices suffered by Catholics, that: 'The subordination of Catholic to Protestant in Derry is a result of force and the threat of force. The condition of Derry may be thought of as one of frozen violence . . . any attempt to thaw it out will liberate violence which is at present static' (*Listener*, 24 October 1968, 526). The forces making for violence in Ulster were, given the background of Irish history, and the existence of the IRA with a base in the South, exceptionally strong. But there is a perennial danger that efforts to promote justice in the face of domination—whether or not these efforts specifically involve illegal disobedience—will evoke violent attempts at repression. However, no political theorist except Hobbes, who is a theorist of absolutism in government, has argued that the possible imprudence of disobedience robs it automatically of moral or political justification.

'Civil disobedience' versus 'resistance'

In fact despite the objections which can be raised against civil disobedience in general, most critics are prepared to allow that certain forms of disobedience may be legitimate. Waldman makes a clear distinction between civil disobedience in the South and the direct action protests against social and economic injustice in the North, reserving much of his criticism for the latter. Kennan objects less to strictly conscientious disobedience than to a strategy of 'confrontation' and provocation. Whilst Lewis Feuer makes a clear distinction between civil disobedience which 'is limited to dramatizing a particular issue; it retains a faith in representative democracy' and civil resistance, which 'is total and unlimited, for it claims that the entire society is corrupt, that representative democracy is a failure, and that the resisters' weapon must be revolutionary' (in Bedau (ed.), *Civil Disobedience*, 204). The distinction is useful, but Feuer's definition of civil resistance is perhaps too extreme. In the discussion that follows it will be used to denote action which is not necessarily revolutionary in intent, but which takes disobedience further than purely *conscientious* objection, or a strict regard for constitutional principles would permit.

There are a series of overlapping points which have been raised to justify conscientious disobedience, but to oppose general resistance. One line of argument bases the right of disobedience on moral principle as interpreted by the individual conscience. Victor Paschkis, a Quaker, writes:

> Civil disobedience is often and seriously misused. It has a place where problems of conscience are involved, and in such cases is a right in the deepest spiritual and religious sense and not a privilege which the secular state, democratic or otherwise, can grant or withhold. Thoreau is an outstanding example (in Kennan, *Democracy and the Student Left*, 121–2).

Where the individual is directly constrained to act contrary to his deepest principles, then he is justified in refusing. But up to that point he should continue to obey the laws of the state as civic duty requires, and should only refuse obedience where his conscience absolutely requires it. This position is taken by Wyzanski, who cites the example of Thomas More, who avoided making a direct challenge to the authority of the king until it was forced upon him. By analogy he concludes that there are not good conscientious grounds for refusing to be drafted into the army, though there may be for refusing actual combat duty in Vietnam. There is certainly no justification in these terms for trespassing on military property or obstructing the Pentagon.

A second line of argument bases the right of civil disobedience less on individual conscience and more on the constitutional position affecting the duties of a citizen. Where the law is positively contrary to the constitution and its principles, as is often the case in the South of the United States, civil disobedience is accepted. But where the law is broken in order to protest against more generalized injustice, then this is not allowable. The remedy lies in the normal constitutional means of effecting change. Or it may be conceded that when laws are flagrantly unjust, even if they can claim to be strictly constitutional, it is right to disobey them. This is the position taken up by Justice Abe Fortas, who concludes:

> In my judgement civil disobedience—the deliberate violation of law—is never justified in our nation where the law being violated is not itself the focus or target of the protest . . . the violation of law merely as a technique of demonstration constitutes an act of rebellion, not merely of dissent (*Concerning Dissent and Civil Disobedience*, 63).

A third approach stresses less the occasion for civil disobedience and more the manner in which it is carried out. It suggests that disobedience is justified if, but only if, legal and political methods of redress have first been exhausted; if civil disobedience is strictly non-violent, if it is openly practised, and if therefore the protesters willingly accept the penalty. The importance of these conditions lies in the fact that their observance makes clear the difference between civil disobedience and ordinary law-breaking, emphasizes the element of moral suasion involved in civil disobedience, reduces the danger of indiscriminate imitation, and is a proof of a basic respect for the constitution and the law. Unless these conditions are fulfilled, even if the initial cause of civil disobedience is just, resort to illegality is not thought to be fully justifiable.

The condition that all constitutional methods of seeking reform should be attempted before breaking the law connects up with another common objection to civil disobedience—an objection which does not deny the hypothetical right of committing civil disobedience, but argues that on political or tactical grounds it is not expedient to resort to it now. The reasons given may be that there is a prospect of improvement after the next election, or as a result of recent legal decisions; or that patience is a necessary virtue in a parliamentary democracy and time is required to convince the majority; or that the pace of reform is satisfactory and opponents must be given time to adjust to the reforms already carried out.

The main rebuttal of these various qualifications surrounding the use of civil disobedience centres on the issue of political relevance. A conception of civil disobedience that circumscribes it purely to individual conscientious objection denies that it is legitimate to seek political aims through this method, and also ensures in practice that civil disobedience will be confined to a sphere of moral purity safely removed from any real impact on public policy. Conscientious objection to participation in war has in the past been allowed in Britain and the United States on religious, but not political, grounds. The Quaker and the Jehovah's Witness are not likely to excite imitation by those not of their religious persuasion; but the man refusing to fight a particular war on political grounds may pave the way for many others to claim the same reason for exemption. He is also challenging the government's authority in a way which the purely religious objector is not. The Supreme Court has, however, recently upheld the American Civil Liberties Union case that conscientious objection should be extended to non-religious objectors and those objecting to a particular war. But if open conscientious objection—or draft-refusal—is the only accepted method of protest then it will tend to be limited to certain sections of the society. If one's main aim is to stop the war, the realistic policy is to promote draft-dodging and desertion, and to protect those who evade the military in these underground ways. This move from civil disobedience to civil resistance is justified, if at all, by the moral and political objections to the particular war—or by a wider political commitment to undermine the state and its military machine in any way possible.

The question of political relevance arises also in connection with the prescription that disobedience should be withheld until the very last moment. If one's aim is to end American pursuit of the war, this aim would best be furthered either by open defiance of the draft, or by organized resistance within the armed forces. Even if an individual objecting to the Vietnam war was sent to serve in Europe, he would be indirectly releasing someone else to fight in Vietnam, and assisting the American military machine. Whilst total consistency in non-co-operation is not possible in any society, the draft is a reasonable and clear-cut point at which to draw the line.

Knowing where to draw the line is important for the individual in knowing when and how to resist. In the case of Thomas More—whose concern was to avoid directly violating his own conscience, but at the same time prudently to avoid open disobedience as long as possible— drawing the line at the last moment was appropriate. But in other circumstances it may be quite inappropriate. A. J. Muste quotes the case of a woman professor of philology in Nazi Germany, who after a while put up a picture of Hitler in her class room, and then after refusing twice to take an oath of allegiance to Hitler, agreed to take it because her students persuaded her she was committing herself to nothing (see Hentoff (ed.), *The Essays of A. J. Muste*, 374). In the case of an objector to the Vietnam war, deciding to withhold obedience only at the point where he was ordered to Vietnam, or into combat, or to shoot civilians, the psychological difficulty of deciding to disobey would almost certainly increase the later he left disobedience, and so would the degree of personal risk involved: that of disobeying orders whilst in action.

The problem of political relevance applies, too, to the distinction between breaking unjust laws in the South and protesting illegally against an unjust situation in the North. Though even in the North it is possible to argue some forms of defiance are constitutional—a New York court accepted the argument that a rent strike could be seen as an appeal to legal processes, since the landlord in violating housing codes had effectively waived the obligation to pay rent—most forms of direct action in Northern cities could not claim constitutional status. Louis Waldman and Abe Fortas both agree that such tactics as blocking council offices or building sites, or sitting down in the streets of New York in the rush hour, are not justified because they are not in direct defiance of unjust laws, and are intentionally disruptive. Fortas stresses the range of constitutional tactics available, including peaceful picketing, and claims that: 'our democratic processes do indeed function', and 'they can bring about fundamental response to fundamental demands, and can do this without revolution' (*Concerning Dissent and Civil Disobedience*, 64).

The central issue is how far normal legal and political processes, which Fortas emphasizes, and purely legal dissent, are effective. William O. Douglas tends to stress instead the comparative powerlessness of the ordinary citizen, especially the poor citizen, to use the courts or the ballot box to defend his basic rights, and the ineffectiveness of constitutional means of protest against the decisions of powerful bureaucracy acting with powerful business interests.

The question of the availability of alternative methods to civil disobedience links up with the question of time. It also illustrates how the constitutionalist position has an inherent conservative bias, whereas support for disobedience and direct action encourages a thorough critique of the economic and political system. It is clear, for example, at the most elementary level of analysis that standard pressure group tactics give an immense advantage to the groups already rich, already influential, and with contacts in Congress and the administration. At election time voting power may count, but only if the community has been mobilized to use this power for its own goals. For a long time the black vote in the Northern cities was largely nullified by being used by the Democratic Party machine. Even when opinion is mobilized, the power of a minority vote is weakened by the fact that Party bosses and national political leaders seek to appeal to a wide range of interest groups, and the least influential count for least provided they can be persuaded to give their votes. (How far a minority group *ought* to influence a democratic process depends on whether it has equal rights under the existing system—this question is taken up in chapter 7.) In the American Party system the range of choices provided by the normal political process to the poorest groups in the community is not wide. On the specific issue of civil rights there has been the additional anomaly that the Democratic Party, which was bidding for black votes in the North, was also the Party of the diehard segregationists of the South. Polarization on the civil rights question has resulted in some shifting of Presidential voting patterns, and has also had an impact on elections and candidates' platforms. But these changes result from the greater degree of awareness and militancy among blacks created by the direct action movement, and later from the city riots. Awareness cannot be created by working through the existing channels, it requires a new movement and forms of combined action. These activities may not necessarily be unconstitutional, but they are necessarily activities outside the Party machine and Congressional lobbies. In terms of the weight they can bring to bear on the political system, the main lever poor blacks have is their power of seizing public attention and of disruption. Since one of the issues is the very high level of unemployment in the ghettos, they do not even have labour's weapon of the strike.

A pure constitutionalist approach is well removed from certain levels of political reality, and projects a highly idealized version of representative democracy. It does not allow for inequal distribution of power and wealth; it does not allow for behind-the-scenes influence; and it tends to ignore the degree of illegal or irregular behaviour within the political system. In the United States corruption within the political parties, within the trade unions, within the administration at all levels, and in Congress has been and still is a fairly normal part of the system. Corruption is also an element in pressure group activity. It is possible to argue that corruption has helped maintain the American form of representative democracy (see Crick, *In Defence of Politics*, 125–6).* It is not possible to argue that corruption is constitutionally legitimate. Moreover, from the viewpoint of groups who have not 'made it' in American society, corruption works against their interests—in the maladministration and diversion of poverty funds, for example.

Moreover, as A. J. Muste cogently argued in 1964, obstructive and unconstitutional tactics can be wielded less visibly, and more effectively, from within the political system than from outside it. He notes that Southern senators 'are presently engaged in the obstructionist tactic of a filibuster'. Muste continues:

> It is usually possible for men in positions of power with the machinery of government in their hands, working to maintain the *status quo*, to obstruct measures they oppose in a respectable and outwardly legal fashion. Southern senators do not have to display themselves on streets in Washington. . . . They do not have to commit 'trespass' or distribute leaflets on the streets, or 'disobey an officer's command.' But the results seen in the Senate today, and the shocking business of these Southern senators being elected to power by a small minority of voters, in direct violation of the Constitution, are no less obstructionist and undemocratic, and even more effective (Hentoff (ed.), *The Essays of A. J. Muste*, 429).

Neither do groups like American negroes or American Indians gain much from the social contract which binds them to the American democracy. In the past, white America has enslaved or killed and dispossessed them; and in the present, they are still largely despised, exploited or dispossessed. They do not enjoy the primitive political blessing of 'law and order' since for the majority of them the white policeman is the man most likely to harass or shoot them. They do in the North enjoy the right to vote without having had to struggle at great personal risk for this privilege. But the blacks living in the decaying slums of the big cities do

---

* See also Robert Merton's analysis of the 'latent functions' of corruption in America in his essay on 'Manifest and latent functions', in R. K. Merton (1957), *Social Theory and Social Structure*, The Free Press, Chicago.

not enjoy decent houses, decent environment, good schools, good jobs, or (often) any jobs. Their poverty is greatly accentuated by the affluence of much of the surrounding society.

In these circumstances the legal niceties of whether a particular form of disobedience can ultimately be justified as constitutional or not, or whether the actual law being broken in a specific protest is in itself a reasonable law, are not seen as particularly relevant. For people who do not feel they are represented adequately, or that they are treated justly, the step from civil disobedience proper to civil resistance is a natural step. Whether it is politically justifiable depends largely on the degree of injustice and degradation being suffered. The militant starts from direct or indirect experience of injustice. The lawyer or constitutional theorist starts from a concern for law and the due political process, which are more immediate to him than an abstract conception of poverty or discrimination. Whether resistance is diverted into political forms, or whether it leads to outright warfare, depends in part on whether the political and administrative processes are flexible enough to adjust to the more pressing demands of the protesters.

Urging patience, because patience is a virtue in representative democracy, is not an answer to the demand for 'freedom now' or 'equality now'. The fact that progress in reform has been made is not in itself enough, if the rate is still so slow that it condemns one to lose the best years of one's life in unemployment, or one's children to grow up in a rat-infested slum. Neither is the fact that a minority of blacks enjoy middle-class jobs, status and education, and suffer rather less overt discrimination, a reason for the majority to be patient. The argument that the time is not ripe for illegal action is equally unconvincing. There are always tactical reasons for discouraging action which might either make things even worse, or else jeopardize the prospects for possible reform. Martin Luther King comments bitterly that:

> Frankly, I have yet to engage in a direct action campaign that was 'well timed' in the view of those who have not suffered unduly from the disease of segregation. For years now I have heard the word 'Wait!' It rings in the ear of every Negro with piercing familiarity. This 'Wait' has almost always meant 'Never' (*Why We Can't Wait*, 80-1).

Patience to a people aware of long oppression is not a virtue but a vice. Patience under insult is not easily compatible with a new-found pride. Pride has in the past been an aristocratic virtue and proud men are always disposed to be troublesome when their dignity is slighted or their liberty at stake. Aristocratic pride underpins the original constitutional achievement of liberty. But when pride spreads among the common people it leads towards increasing democracy—and often clashes with the constitutional order benefiting the upper classes. When the vote has been extended but democracy is still contained within the former representative system, the groups still excluded from any real representation or equality will, once politically mobilized, make new demands.

Different considerations apply to disobedience, often by the more privileged sections of the community, which is designed to alter government military policies. When a war is being waged, as in Vietnam, questions concerning the constitutional status of the war or whether it has majority support are, though important, secondary. The central issue is whether the war is a just war, and whether it is being waged by legitimate means. The appeal here must necessarily be beyond the internal constitution of the state to wider principles of international law or general morality.

Counsels of patience are, in the context of a war in which people are being killed daily, particularly inappropriate. Resisters to the war in Vietnam often invoke the example of Nazi Germany. Noam Chomsky writes: 'What justifies an act of civil disobedience is an intolerable evil. After the lessons of Dachau and Auschwitz, no person of conscience can believe that authority must always be obeyed' (in Bedau (ed.), *Civil Disobedience*, 202). Lewis Feuer takes some justifiable exception to the emotive vagueness of the comparison with the resistance to Hitler, arguing that the European resistance movements were 'fighting the Nazis who had abrogated all constitutional processes, banned the opposition parties, and imprisoned their leaders. It makes no sense to describe the American democracy in such terms' (ibid., 205). But he ignores the central point that the most serious charge against Nazi Germany was not that it was a dictatorship, but that it murdered millions of Jews and brutally subjugated other countries by force. The massacre of civilians is not made legitimate if committed under the auspices of a constitutional government. This point was made by proponents of civil disobedience against nuclear policies. Bertrand Russell wrote: 'The governments of East and West calmly contemplate the possibility of a massacre at least a hundred times greater than that perpetrated by Hitler' (in Urquhart (ed.), *A Matter of Life*, 195). Robert Bolt argued that: 'It is not impossible for a democratically elected government to enact wicked laws' (ibid., 45). The comparison with Nazi Germany made by resisters to the Vietnam war can be more directly sustained by appealing to evidence of the methods of warfare used in Vietnam. The evidence available since the mid-1960s, but now more openly and authoritatively publicized, suggests that the comparison is not as absurd as Americans would wish.

The most publicized American war crime has been the My Lai massacre of 1968. An army-initiated enquiry under General Peers recommended that charges of covering up the incident be laid against fifteen officers. Most of the report of the Peers Commission was not published. A *New York Times* leak in 1972 revealed that the division commander had suppressed evidence of the massacre. A book by Seymour Hersh based on the complete transcript of the findings of the Peers Commission (*Cover-up*) suggests that My Lai was an extreme but not exceptional case—one hundred civilians were killed the same morning in the village of My Khe, a mile away from My Lai. An Episcopalian chaplain with the American division told the Peers Commission: 'I became absolutely convinced that as far as the American Army was concerned there was no such thing as murder of a Vietnamese civilian' (*The Times*, 19 January 1972, p. 1). A report by the American Friends Service Committee, presented to the White House, documented the following charges:

> Americans have knowingly funded and accepted as instruments of national policy: i) Undeclared war; ii) The most intensive and indiscriminate bombing in history; iii) The use of bombing to destroy civilian society where this seemed necessary to drive out the guerrilla forces; iv) The calculated and planned use of political assassination; v) The declaration of up to half a country as a 'free fire zone'; vi) The use of defoliation and herbicides as weapons of war on a massive scale; vii) The forced emigration of peasants to cities by means of saturation bombing and evacuation at gun point; viii) The daily announcement of a body count as a barometer of national success (*Indochina 1971*, 16–18).

A macabre footnote to this last point was provided by the court martial of Lieutenant Duffy who was charged with ordering the killing of an unarmed Vietnamese prisoner who had been found hiding. Duffy's defence, supported by four other lieutenants from his battalion, was that he understood the 'body count' was a measure of military success, and their instructions were to take no prisoners in combat. The military court revoked an initial conviction of 'murder', found Duffy guilty of involuntary manslaughter, and sentenced him to six months' imprisonment.

The point where it is justifiable to move from limited civil disobedience to sustained civil resistance is determined in part by the nature of the government and representative system. Therefore, as suggested earlier, the more groups of people are excluded in a representative system from real representation, or from the other benefits accruing from citizenship, the less obligation they feel, or can be expected to feel, to accept the rules of the constitution. But even if all constitutional blessings accrue to protesters, they will be justified in opposing certain situations of extreme injustice or inhumanity—and in doing so could appeal to the natural law principles underlying constitutionalist theory. Noam Chomsky comments that: 'The limits of civil disobedience must be determined by the extent of the evil that one confronts, and by considerations of tactical efficiency and moral principle' (in Bedau (ed.), *Civil Disobedience*, 202). The step from civil disobedience to resistance may be justified either in the constitutional terms just defined, or by a theoretical rejection of constitutionalism for another conception of democracy, equality and individual rights.

The demands of realism

The conflict between adherents of parliamentary democracy and between those who reject it can be resolved, if at all, only in the compass of a wide-ranging examination of the values, goals and institutions involved in the constitutionalist and more radical democratic viewpoints. But laying aside the argument from the values of representative democracy, Kennan goes on to attack civil disobedience or resistance from the standpoint of its political effectiveness—in fact for tactical reasons. He comments:

> The history of American political thought contains no more moving and noble vision of individual freedom than Thoreau's great essay. And yet . . . Thoreau's words and actions were an embarrassment to his more prominent and influential friends in the abolitionist movement—men whose voices were at that time more important to the advancement of the cause than his own (*Democracy and the Student Left*, 214).

Kennan adds that the Mexican War was not ended by civil disobedience, and that the Civil War which ended slavery did not resolve the problems of American negroes, thus Thoreau's belief in simple solutions was misguided. The conception of realism which underlies this criticism is one based on the idea of statesmanship—awareness of the responsibilities facing men in power, the complexities which they face, and the need often to choose between evils, to compromise and to play for time.

It is a view of politics which is naturally different from that of the individual dissenter looking at issues from the distance of detached individual judgment, and in terms of general principles rather than immediate practicalities; and which sees individual responsibility in terms not of decision making but of dissent. The more the dissenter is guided by his conscience and the less account he takes of specifically political considerations, the less likely is his action to have any immediate political effect. It is certainly true that Thoreau's action had no bearing at all on the Mexican war—though his essay has had a continuing long-term influence. But apart from writing his essay he took no active steps to promote disobedience, or to organize political opposition or resistance. As we have seen earlier, when disobedience is used as a tactic by a movement mobilizing mass support, constitutionalist critics tend to object to it as moving beyond the sphere of legitimate protest. An individual moral gesture can be admired for its rare qualities, whilst the dissenter is simultaneously patronized for his unworldliness, and relegated, as it were, to the status of a museum piece, a beautiful irrelevance to everyday life. Nevertheless, political realism underrates the power of example, especially of true heroism or martyrdom (Thoreau was not called on to display the first or suffer the second). As sometimes happens with ideas, there are times when individual example can spark off a dangerous blaze, and threaten the established order. The dissenter may also at times have greater effect on public policy than his more discreet and influential friends. Active dissent which takes embarrassing forms shifts the focus and scope of debate, and opens up possibilities previously unreal. The limits of political realism are intangible, and closely linked to general opinion. Under the impetus of an influential movement, what was unthinkable may become possible, and then necessary; and the power of any movement depends not only on its numbers and its ability to enforce its demands, but on the strength of its determination and the inspiration of its ideals.

The archetype of morally based civil disobedience is Antigone. And she also illustrates the disastrous effects moral absolutism may have when it clashes with the demands of political order. Conor Cruise O'Brien comments in a reflection on Antigone: 'Peace depends on the acceptance of civil subordination, since the powerful will use force to uphold their laws: the perpetual assertion of a higher law is therefore a principle of permanent revolution' (*Listener*, 24 October 1968, 526). O'Brien concludes that the world would be a more peaceful place without the element Antigone brings to political life, but that what would be lost is intangible —'a way of imagining and dramatising man's dignity'. O'Brien ends his thoughts on a note of romantic ambivalence, aware of the case for obedience, but fundamentally on the side of Antigone. Antigone and Creon symbolize the dangers of uncalculating adherence to moral principle on the one hand and brutal repression on the other. But the dilemma is not necessarily as great as in the tragedy, because as O'Brien notes, both Antigone and Creon are extremely rash. It is not impossible for dissent to be combined with a degree of prudence. It is possible too, as O'Brien also notes, that where the government is sufficiently rash, disobedience is the path of discretion as well as valour; and disobedience may encourage a more prudent and conciliatory ruler to take over in order to preserve a semblance of order. Alternatively, where Creon is behaving with sufficient restraint, Antigone either will not be provoked to action—or if she is, her case may be less attractive than it normally is.

It is the latter position that Kennan assumes holds good in the United States today, a moderate government faced with unjustified disobedience. Despite his gibe at Thoreau's ineffectiveness, Kennan is, like many others, mainly concerned that morally based disobedience will (even if it does not attain its goal) be too effective in disturbing the public peace. He makes plain that in the potential conflict between justice and order, he comes down on the side of the latter.

Yet it is perfectly clear from the wider context of Kennan's writings that he is defending not any order, but the imperfect order of a constitutional state endowed with national independence and a representative democracy. He is, moreover, extremely concerned about the individual's claim to dignity. He is, therefore, giving priority to order not only for the sake of peace, and its very real blessings, but for the sake of the justice so far achieved and precariously maintained. The real conflict is not between justice and order in the abstract, but between those who believe it is possible and necessary to seek greater justice, and greater dignity for those denied it, by means similar to the turbulence that secured constitutional democracy, and those who fear this attempt will forfeit what has been gained.

6 Direct action and liberal values

The liberalism embodied in liberal democracy is linked both to the constitutional heritage of the rule of law and parliamentary institutions, and to a democratic belief in the acceptance of the majority will. But the central concerns of liberalism have been with individual and minority rights on the one hand, and the values of freedom, rationality and toler-ance on the other. These values are guarantees of individualism, and to be desired for their own sake.

The belief in individualism involves seeking the maximum area of free choice and action compatible with an orderly society, and minimizing not only the governmental or social restraints on action, but also any external intrusion on individual privacy. The most crucial freedoms of all are those which concern individual thought and speech, freedom of discussion among friends, and freedom of conscience and worship. Beyond these are the political freedoms necessary to realize fully individual freedom and to maintain a liberal society: freedom to speak publicly, to assemble together, to publish what one wishes, to petition the government. Constitutionalism and liberalism coincide in their emphasis on the importance of these political liberties, and on the need to avoid state intrusion into the realm of personal privacy. This sense of privacy is summed up in the commonplace phrase that 'an Englishman's home is his castle'. Liberal thinkers have, however, gone further in stressing the rights of individualism against the tyranny of social fashion and censure—the right to dress differently, to act differently, to be eccentric, and even to be 'immoral' within the law. Political differences, and religious or social differences, can only be preserved if the rights not only of the indivi-dual, but of minorities, are respected—since the individual cannot en-joy fully his freedom unless he can associate with other like-minded individuals.

Concern for freedom is very closely associated in liberalism with respect for rationality. Belief that men are, or are potentially, reasonable beings is a justification for giving them a degree of liberty which might otherwise be dangerous to political order. Reason is also the attribute of any mature individual, a justification of faith in individualism, since reason and morality are believed to be closely allied. In the classic liberal defence of freedom, John Stuart Mill's 'On Liberty', it is not so much freedom itself that is extolled, as freedom which is the midwife of reason. Freedom of thought and speech enables the progress of civilization, since error is corrigible by reason, and the rational must, in the long-run, prevail if the truth is not suppressed.

Individual privacy and minority rights require buttressing by another liberal value, that of tolerance. Passionate conviction of sin or of social danger is conducive to the tyranny of opinion. Religious freedom or sexual freedom can only be granted where there is a degree of tolerance of differing religious beliefs and practices or differing sexual codes of behaviour. Similarly, political differences of opinion will only be allowed genuine freedom of expression where there is a tolerance of political diversity, both by the government and the population as a whole. Indeed, this tolerance maintains the acceptance of the rules of parliamentary government—though custom and respect for the constitution may be more important in this respect. Tolerance is also necessary to enable rational discourse, since it implies not only a willingness to let others speak, but to listen to them and so remain open to a degree of persuasion.

Direct action appears as a threat to liberal values primarily because it seems to represent a degree of irrationalism and intolerance—an abandonment of reasoned argument for emotional appeals or direct coercion, an impatience with the normal political processes, and a conviction of rightness which justifies the methods used.

But the case either for or against direct action depends primarily on the context in which action is taken; on the prevalence of tolerance, on the role of reason within the existing political process, and on the degree of freedom which exists. The liberal usually applauds dissenters in an illiberal regime who claim the right to free, critical speech; to publish and to circulate subversive literature; to demonstrate peaceably in the streets; and to flout police restrictions on these activities. When dissenters attack the practices of press censorship, restrictions on personal freedom of movement and police intrusion into individual privacy, they are seen as upholding liberal goals against dictatorship or 'totalitarianism'. Therefore, the first and most important question to be considered is whether the liberal democracies of the West are indeed genuinely free societies which uphold the liberal ideal.

In critiques of liberal society, for example, by the New Left in the 1960s, three distinct positions emerge: that civil liberties have been limited and eroded; or that the liberties exist, but have been rendered ineffective; or that they serve as a diversion from the underlying realities of repression. These analyses also lead to differing conclusions about direct action. If civil liberties have been curtailed (or never in reality existed), then direct action may be seen as a means of reasserting or creating these liberties necessary to a liberal society. Direct action becomes a method of fulfilling liberal values, as it has often been in the historical evolution of parliamentary liberalism. If, on the other hand, liberties do exist, but are ineffective, direct action is used as an extension of freedom of dissent to make dissent effective—and becomes in fact an attempt to increase democracy. If existing freedoms are regarded as a means of manipulation, direct action will probably be used as an instrument of 'confrontation' to unmask the repressiveness of the existing system, and as a prelude to a hoped for revolution.

One difficulty in considering these interpretations is that of generalization. A strong selective case can be made that liberal democracies fail to live up to their declared ideal of political freedom by adding up bad examples from different countries. But concrete examples of illiberalism stem often from distinct historical and cultural causes—a legacy of fascism, a particularly exposed position in the cold war, or a specific crisis like the war in Algeria. The following discussion is confined to the United States and Britain—usually held up as prototypes of parliamentary liberalism. America is an obvious model for generalizing about western society. But comparison with Britain should help to illustrate the influence of specifically American factors upon the condition of American freedoms.

The erosion of civil liberties

There are two levels of political freedom—freedom to express personal non-conformity and dissent in the private sphere of the home, the local club, or at work; and freedom for active and public dissent designed to influence government policy. The first form of freedom, which is related to the basic guarantees of individual liberty contained in the right to privacy, is sometimes compatible with autocratic forms of government—for example, with Hobbes's conception that liberty lies in the 'silence of the laws'. This is the kind of freedom guaranteed in a constitutional state which may not invoke liberal or democratic values. Personal freedom to dissent is logically a prerequisite of public freedom to protest, and is further reinforced by open expression of dissent—the defence of civil liberties involves defending both types of freedom. But the two spheres may be separable, not only because individual dissent may be tolerated by autocratic governments, but more paradoxically, because public dissent may be constitutionally allowed at the same time as considerable pressure is brought to bear upon individuals to conform, and the right to privacy is denied.

The pressure towards conformity springs chiefly from the demands of 'security' which have been predominant since the Second World War. Invasion of individual privacy by the security services does not affect all citizens equally. It impinges mainly on two quite distinct categories—on people whose jobs have security implications, and on those who have chosen to express some form of dissent from mainstream political opinion. The former case primarily involves issues of personal freedom and personal rights, the latter has more direct bearing on the reality of the right to public dissent.

Security probes extend most rigorously to those who have chosen to serve the government by entering into the civil service or into forms of industrial or scientific work covered by official security. A National Council for Civil Liberties pamphlet comments that in Britain 'security' has provided a new kind of crime. 'There are no precise charges in security procedures, no judicial processes, and the penalties are normally loss of employment and destruction of career' (*Handbook of Citizens' Rights*, 35). An individual who is found to have held communist sympathies is not given any clear indication why he is convicted as unreliable, and in some cases the reasons may be extremely tenuous. Firms working on government contracts also have to act against individuals found by the government security officers to be a security risk. In 1956 ICI had to dismiss a solicitor because his wife was a former member of the Communist Party.

Screening in the United States has been conducted through security hearings as well as behind-the-scenes investigation. Justice Douglas comments on the security hearings of federal and state employees, and of those working for contractors or subcontractors on defence, that by 1970 at least twenty million people had gone through security hearings (though the scope of those covered has varied with Presidential rulings and Supreme Court adjudication on the issue). Douglas writes:

> The casualties have been staggering in the past and they continue to mount. . . . The hearings seldom dealt with overt acts against the United States. They probed thoughts, attitudes and beliefs. At various times a man was suspect—and often suspended—if he believed in the U.N., if he thought schools should be segregated, if he thought Peking should be admitted to the U.N. . . . In the sixties employees were still being screened for association with so-called communist 'front' organizations, not especially present associations but associations dating way in the past when friendship with Russia, welded in World War II, was considered a national virtue (*Points of Rebellion*, 17–20).

Security hearings by loyalty boards are, Douglas argues, a powerful force for encouraging conformity in political, intellectual and even cultural interests. (Speaking Russian or owning Paul Robeson records could be a sign of pro-Communist sympathies in the eyes of many tribunals.) Legislative security hearings by HUAC and its sister committee in the Senate were in the 1950s also a potent means of discouraging dissent among the public at large, since any member of a protest organization, or any individual who fell under suspicion could be ordered to appear before the committee, and could lose his reputation and his job. Since the power of the committees depends largely on the prevailing political climate, in the 1960s they were forced on to the defensive by the greater willingness of their victims to challenge their authority, by decreasing willingness of courts to sustain contempt-citations, or of Congress to vote funds to the committees, and by less willingness on the part of the public to take them seriously.

One of the most damaging aspects of the McCarthy era, which was related to the ethos of loyalty hearings and legislative investigations, but did not directly depend on them, was a tendency to fire individuals suspected of dissident views or associations, and to get them blacklisted for further jobs. The effects of blacklisting (sometimes totally arbitrary or even based on confusion between surnames) lasted in, for example, the film industry long after McCarthyism had disappeared. Neither is this kind of sanction necessarily a relic of the 1950s. Observers have noted a recent revival of political discrimination in the academic world. Noam Chomsky said in June 1971 that: 'In the past year there has been a rash of firings, mostly at smaller colleges and universities, on what appear to be strictly political grounds' (*Problems of Knowledge and Freedom*, 59). Banning political dissidents from teaching in higher education has obvious implications for intellectual and academic freedom as well as personal and political liberty.

Another sanction attaching to the open avowal of dissident opinions is that it lays both organizations and individuals open to surveillance by the security services. Moreover, whilst the powers of public hearings decrease during periods of widespread protest activity, the power of the security services may in fact increase, and the scope of surveillance be extended to maintain a check on all potentially 'dangerous' groups.

Although the main targets of security probes are potentially subversive groups, certain security checks entail an indiscriminate and wholesale inspection of private communications. For example, a *Daily Express* article of February 1967 revealed that commercial and private cables sent from Britain were regularly sent to the Ministry of Defence for analysis. It is reasonable to assume that international phone calls are similarly monitored. A *Sunday Times* article of 20 June 1971, pointed out:

> Last year students in Copenhagen found a telephone monitoring station in the University basement. According to reports in the Danish paper, Politiken, 50 Danish Post Office men were employed in five centres, recording trunk calls out of Denmark for NATO Intelligence. If that goes on in peaceful Denmark, it is hardly likely that it is not done here (49).

Legally tapping internal telephone calls and opening personal mail requires the issue of a warrant by the Home Secretary. But a Post Office employee told the Hampstead Group of the Committee of 100 that in his postal district there were blanket interceptions 'when, on certain days, all the mail of foreign students attending a college of further education would go "Upstairs" to be opened'. The Committee's pamphlet concludes that mail is often intercepted without a formal warrant. Another Post Office

worker asked to comment on the pamphlet wrote: 'Times of civil distur-
bance and political fermentation are the signal, in my experience, for
great activity in letter opening and telephone tapping. In my own area,
local Communists and students at the . . . college are constant victims'
(*Mail Interception and Telephone Tapping in Britain*, 5). Another Post
Office informant suggested in *Solidarity* that there were regular checks
at intervals, at an estimated average of twenty-five lines per exchange
per week.

Formal warrants for phone tapping and opening letters increased
between 1936 and 1956, according to the Birkett Report of 1957, and
fourteen government agencies secured warrants. Since 1957 the government has refused to reveal figures (see Thompson, *Big Brother in Britain
Today*, 125–6). The fact that the *Railway Gazette* had its phone tapped
at the end of 1972, after leaking government plans for railway closures,
suggests that the practice is now widespread.

An additional check on dissidents is the photographing of demonstrations. A number of protests were made about police photographing
members of perfectly legal CND marches—for example, a north-west
CND march to Barrow in 1964, when the police were pressurized by
public protests into destroying the negatives. Peter Hain noted police
photographed Stop the Seventies Tour demonstrators. The police have
also taken the registration numbers of cars at CND meetings.

Another way of discovering potential trouble makers is to recruit
informers inside colleges and universities. The *Daily Telegraph* reported in
June 1968 that a Persian student at London University had claimed the
police approached him to ask for co-operation in passing on information,
and had been surprised when he refused:

> They said that they had interviewed many students about the same
> thing and had never had a reception like this before. All they
> wanted were the names of any radical students known to me in the
> college, of any nationality, not just foreigners—and forewarning of
> any demonstrations or political activities (ibid., 70).

Complaints about the recruitment of spies reached the National Union
of Students from a range of other colleges and universities.

The FBI also investigates student activities both to vet prospective
employees in 'sensitive' jobs, and on a more routine scale. 'The Golden
Gator of San Francisco State University reported that some twenty-five
security agents visited the university each semester, checking on the
background and affiliations of fifty or more students' (Cook, *The FBI
Nobody Knows*, 398). It was discovered at Yale in December 1962 that a
former FBI agent, who had become the University Security Director and
Associate Dean of Students, had been compiling security files on both
staff and students.

There are no legal restrictions on the British government's exercise of its powers to invade individual privacy. In theory there are greater legal safeguards in the United States—though the 1968 Omnibus Crime Control and Safe Streets Act abandoned many of these safeguards. Edwin Newman, the author of a legal guide to *Civil Liberty and Civil Rights* comments that this Act: 'authorized eavesdropping at all levels of government, federal and state, for a designated group of suspected crimes, but with the requirement that it be court authorized, except in matters of national security, where the executive branch could authorize' (47). The Act broadened the definition of national security to cover domestic political actions 'to attack and subvert the government by unlawful means'. Prior to this Act, however, the FBI did tap without legal authorization. Former FBI agent Jack Levine reported:

> It is a matter of common knowledge among the Bureau's Agents that much of the wiretapping done by the field offices is not reported to the Bureau. This is the result of the pressure for convictions. A still greater number of taps are not reported by the Bureau to the Attorney General or to the Congress (Cook, *The FBI Nobody Knows*, 24–5).

Levine also stated on a radio broadcast that the FBI opens mail, though 'neither the Post Office Department nor the FBI likes to advertise the fact that this is going on'.

Evidence has also recently come to light of extremely extensive spying upon political figures, including members of Congress, by the security services of the armed forces. Senate hearings early in 1971 revealed that over a two year period, the army collected information on 18,000 civilians. A former member of counter-intelligence testified that in 1967 and 1968 he was directed to start a 'left-wing intelligence desk': 'I was literally to cover all aspects of left-wing activity in the United States', he said, explaining that every day he would receive 'thousands of FBI reports and a great number of military intelligence reports on groups and persons engaged in dissident activity'. Most of them were then microfilmed in Washington (*The Times*, 25 February 1971, 7).

The extent of police and military probing into the private lives and political activities of those openly expressing dissent undermines genuine freedom of political opinion and dissent. The fact that public avowal of unorthodox views may result in a substantial invasion of one's privacy is in itself a deterrent—though many people probably realize this too late. An even greater hazard attaching to membership of groups held particularly suspect by the police is that one lays oneself open to police harassment. In Britain this has so far taken relatively minor forms. For example, after the bombing of the home of the Minister of Employment and Productivity in 1970 police searched two hundred homes and took in for questioning members of diverse organizations including members of Women's Liberation. After the IRA bomb attack on Aldershot in 1972 the police raided the homes of several International Socialists and took away material irrelevant to Ireland. In the United States police have preferred serious 'criminal' charges against political activists—drugs charges are particularly convenient. For example, John Sinclair, an organizer for the White Panther Party in Detroit was sentenced in July 1969 to nine-and-a-half years in jail for giving two marijuana cigarettes to a police agent posing as a friend. In Houston, Texas, a former SNCC field secretary was sentenced to *thirty* years' imprisonment for possession of one joint of marijuana; police picked him up two days after he had publicly criticized the local mayor and police chief (see Davis, *If They Come in the Morning . . .*, 95).

Extensive police surveillance not only erodes existing freedoms, it also establishes practices which could be developed into a fully-fledged police state apparatus. The Nixon administration moved in this direction when it claimed that police had eavesdropped on a member of the Black Panthers in order to protect 'national security', and therefore was not obliged to disclose in court what had been overheard. The Appeals Judge observed that such a doctrine would allow the Justice Department to 'ride roughshod over numerous political freedoms which have long received constitutional protection'. In this case the Judge ordered the evidence to be disclosed. But the Deputy Attorney General explained to the press that: 'You can't divide subversion into two parts—domestic and foreign.' He concluded that dissident domestic organizations should be treated like agents of hostile powers (*Progressive*, April 1971, 27–8).

Legislative trends in America in the late 1960s marked an increasing threat to both civil liberties and political freedom of dissent. The 1968 Federal Anti-Riot Act, which was tacked on to the 1968 Civil Rights Law, provided penalties for those who cross state lines to foment riots. The Chicago Conspiracy Trial was based on this Act. In November 1969 the FBI announced they would investigate whether organizers of the peaceful November Moratorium demonstration against the Vietnam War had violated the Act. Legislation to enable preventive detention prior to their trial of prisoners charged with a range of violent crimes was put before Congress. A suspect certified by the government to be 'a likely danger to the Community' could be denied bail. Without the benefit of such legislation courts refused to allow bail to Black Panthers in a number of cases where, after being in prison for up to two years, the charges against them were dismissed.

Provisions also exist for political internment in a time of emergency. The FBI has plans for an 'Operation Dragnet', which entails rounding up and detaining in camps everyone on its list of Communist Party members. One of the clauses of the McCarran Act which has not been ruled unconstitutional by the Supreme Court (in its nature it has not yet been invoked) provides for detention camps in times of emergency, and potential detention camps exist. The House of Representatives delayed a bill before it in 1970 to repeal this statute of the McCarran Act until the bill was lost, though it had been passed by the Senate. The possibility of internment being introduced as an instrument of government policy cannot be lightly dismissed either, after British troops implemented internment in Ulster in August 1971, rounding up in the process people with no proven connections with the IRA.

Despite the indirect threat posed by the prevalence of police state methods of spying on supposedly subversive or dangerous dissenters, and despite the selective repression of certain black and radical groups in the USA, direct restrictions on the freedom of political organization and protest have been fairly rare. A number of restrictive measures taken against the American Communist Party, and supposed 'front' organizations, in the 1950s were ruled unconstitutional by the Supreme Court in the 1960s. The Court decided the government had no right to require the registration of Communist organizations, to withhold passports from American citizens because of their political affiliations, or to make citizens request formal permission to receive certain foreign publications. The Court also amended the interpretation of the Smith Act, which sent eleven Communist Party leaders to prison for advocating the overthrow of the government, although in 1951 the Court had upheld their conviction.

Restrictions on the First Amendment freedoms of free speech, assembly and procession, when they occur, take the form of police exercising their discretion and of invoking local regulations. This has happened most frequently in the South. But Hayden argues that in 1968, Chicago city officials 'refused to engage in serious negotiations over permits until one week before the Convention, when we sued them in federal Court'. Earlier they had refused proposals for a Festival of Life and a march to the Democratic Convention on grounds of 'security' and 'traffic congestion' (*Trial*, 45–6).

In Britain, where there is no constitutional *right* of public protest, the restrictions applied also stem from local bylaws and police decisions. People have been arrested for obstruction for trying to make a public speech in certain places. Sellers of minority newspapers have also been arrested for obstruction, when vendors of national newspapers on the same spot were not. The police may, and often do, prescribe a route to avoid disorder.

The ineffectiveness of political freedoms

Hayden argues that Chicago provided a 'casebook example of the difference between real and empty constitutional rights'. He is not, however, arguing that the liberty to dissent does not exist, but that this liberty as it stands is meaningless, because constitutional dissent is wholly ineffective. He writes:

> When the democratic system is less than pure, when in fact it is corrupt, then First Amendment rights are ineffective and citizens have to return to the *origins* of the First Amendment and rediscover their own sovereignty. . . . We are in a condition in which the First Amendment freedoms do not work effectively. Citizens have the right to speak, assemble, and protest freely until their actions begin to have a subversive effect on unresponsive authorities (ibid., 44–5).

The existing liberties, in this view, far from providing a means for relevant political dissent, simply serve as safety valves for letting off steam— instead of being truly political liberties, they are rather an extension of private freedom, a space for individual self-expression safely removed from the sphere of public policy, but creating an illusion of political activity. Hannah Arendt suggests in her study *On Violence* that the reason why some student radicals have rejected liberal freedoms is that they 'no longer open the channels for action, for the meaningful extension of freedom' (81). But Hayden is arguing not so much that liberal freedoms are *inherently* ineffective or meaningless, but rather that they exist within an inegalitarian and undemocratic political system which renders the ordinary citizen impotent.

Two strategies emerge from the previous discussion—one defensive and the other offensive. Where the liberty of political dissent is being restricted, then the best way to defend constitutional liberties is to practise them despite restrictions.

The Wobblies's Free Speech Campaigns would fall into this category; so would the 1964 Berkeley Free Speech Movement protests against university restrictions on political activity, like giving out political literature on the campus. Direct action against institutions which promote illiberalism also falls into this category. A statement of American New Left attitudes in 1961, which comments that contemporary liberalism 'no longer even *is* liberalism in our sense', emphasizes the importance of demonstrations against the House UnAmerican Activities Committee by students in San Francisco in 1960 (Jacobs and Landau, *The New Radicals*, 105–6).

Where the constitutional freedoms do exist, but seem ineffective, then it is relevant to try to extend their limits and to increase their impact. This approach may, like the first, result in challenging restrictions on the place of assembly or route of a march—as the Chicago demonstrators did when they refused to be sealed off from the actual Democratic Convention. Asserting civil liberties merges into seeking increased political effectiveness in some instances. But a point is reached where action cannot be defended in terms of maintaining constitutional rights of protest, and becomes a form of deliberate civil disobedience or a direct challenge to particular policies or institutions.

An attempt to increase the power of ordinary citizens within liberal democracy may mean opposing not only the government but the power of business corporations who influence policy. 'Liberalism' is associated not only with a genuine development of personal and political freedom, but also with the evolution of a capitalist economy. In its past and present associations with 'freedom' for private enterprise 'liberalism' is necessarily seen as a largely hypocritical doctrine, which may be used to disguise policies depriving large numbers of people of their freedom and autonomy. The Students for a Democratic Society identified the main enemy as 'corporate liberalism', and attacked the 'respectable people' who in Hayden's words are linked to 'the foundations, corporations and banks and the Democratic Party, who parade in their own suburban communities as liberals, but who happen to own lock, stock and barrel, the major enterprises in Mississippi' (ibid., 42–3).

The implications of 'confrontation'

The early New Left made a distinction between the validity of universalized liberal values and the ideological and propaganda uses of liberal clichés to promote particular interests. If, however, existing political liberties and liberal values are seen primarily as part of a system of manipulation—as they tended to be by the later New Left, there is logic in a political strategy which seeks by continuous confrontation to provoke the authorities into revealing the underlying repressiveness of the system. This is suggested by Herbert Marcuse in his essay on 'Repressive tolerance':

> The exercise of political rights (such as voting, letter-writing to the press, to Senators, etc., protest-demonstrations with a prior renunciation of counter-violence) in a society of total administration serves to strengthen this administration by testifying to the existence of democratic liberties which, in reality, have changed their content and lost their effectiveness. In such a case, freedom (of opinion, of assembly, of speech) becomes an instrument for absolving servitude (in Wolff, *et al.*, *A Critique of Pure Tolerance*, 98).

Marcuse argues, as did student radicals adopting his theory, that violence is necesssry to oppose this manipulative system. Gareth Stedman Jones, for example, comments on the awakening of the Left to the nature of its 'liberal, pluralist democracy' as a result of the Vietnam war:

> Its parliamentary institutions became seen as a screen for manipulation and oppression—its formal freedoms as themselves an

instrument for deadening popular consciousness and dissent. 'Repressive tolerance', in Marcuse's words, was the key to the political structure which had stifled all unrest within late capitalism. Thus, for the student generation of the 1960s, it suddenly became clear that violence could have a liberating purpose (in Cockburn and Blackburn (eds.), *Student Power*, 38).

In considering the implications of 'confrontation' both the purpose of the strategy and the methods used are relevant. Confrontation was an element in earlier civil rights protests, dramatizing for the nation and the world the repressive violence used by Southern police and white mobs to keep blacks in their place. Though the demonstrations involved a degree of 'provocation', they served primarily to publicize the habitual level of violence used against blacks, and especially blacks trying to assert their rights. Moreover, since the demonstrations were intended to claim basic constitutional rights, and were conducted peacefully, the violence of the response was clearly not justified by the demonstrators' own actions.

Confrontation designed to expose repressive tolerance cannot in itself expose the mechanisms of manipulation, only the forces of repression. While the experience of police brutality may lead those involved, and those sympathetic to them, to look with new eyes at political authority, it will not necessarily have that effect on the majority. Indeed, the more efficient the manipulative techniques, the more effectively will they isolate radical opposition (as Marcuse recognizes) and justify violence used by the authorities.

A strategy of confrontation has inherent difficulties—whether the methods used are violent or peaceful—whenever the 'violence' which is being exposed is not the immediate violence of a police state or of crude colonial domination, but the inequality and repression institutionalized in the economic and political system, or the potential mass violence of military preparations. The institutional involvement of universities in defence research, for example, is not directly exposed if the police are called in to quell a demonstration on the campus. The existence of a level of desperate poverty within an affluent society is not directly exposed by a bomb explosion. And even where violence is being practised on a massive scale in an actual war, if the war is far away the violence is not necessarily made more visible by demonstrators storming the Pentagon or the American Embassy. If confrontation is intended as a form of political dramatization, then the use of violence by the demonstrators, even on a minor scale, tends to distract attention from the central issue. Moreover, in a society where economic inequalities and political bias are widely accepted by prevailing opinion, and there is a genuine tradition of political liberty, confrontation tactics may create a repressive response from authorities normally permissive.

If violence is used not as a tactic of confrontation, but as a means of direct resistance to a specific policy or to the regime as a whole, then its political rationale is different. It is not clear from Marcuse's own essay whether he sees violence primarily as a means of confrontation or of resistance. Towards the end of his discussion of repressive tolerance he in fact suggests the latter: 'there is a "natural right" of resistance for oppressed and overpowered minorities to use extralegal means if the legal ones have proved to be inadequate. . . . If they use violence, they do not start a new chain of violence but try to break an established one' (in Wolff, et al., A Critique of Pure Tolerance, 130–1). In this case violent resistance is an extension of the existing forms of dissent rather than a specific attempt to expose the sham of liberal freedom and tolerance— and may be justified if the cause for resistance is serious enough, and if violence is likely to be effective. Violent resistance may result in restrictions of political freedom, but it does so as the byproduct of the struggle rather than as a prelude to real resistance, as is the case in deliberate provocation by a small minority. Whether or not violent resistance is likely to be effective depends partly on the conditions discussed in chapter 4, and whether the violence is an extension of a genuine popular movement among at least a section of the population, and hence politically significant.

If violent confrontation is adopted from a position of relative weakness, with the implicit aim of forcing the government into revoking existing liberties and being overtly repressive, then it is likely to be self-defeating if not disastrous. The movement itself will be very considerably hampered if it is forced to work underground—these difficulties have been experienced by the Weathermen. Even if freedom to speak, assemble, organize, and demonstrate do not result in any immediate impact on public policy they are prerequisites for building up a long-term movement. Second, success in promoting a repressive backlash will damage all other groups engaged in forms of opposition, and weaken the civil liberties which do exist for society as a whole. In addition wherever the administration is responding repressively to dissent, as in the imprisonment and trumped-up charges against black leaders and anti-war demonstrators between 1968 and 1971 in the United States, then the opposition needs the protection still to some extent afforded by freedom to propagandize and by the courts. Furthermore, if there is a trend towards fascism, which Marcuse was forecasting in American society in 1970, the most urgent requirement is the development of a common front of liberal and left forces.

Where the immediate aim is not to promote conditions for revolution but to resist a particular policy, the radical opposition needs the informal or even formal assistance of more influential groups within the mass media, legislature and the administration. Hayden proposed in 1969 that attempts should be made to enlist support from liberal elements in the establishment to slow down the repression of the Panthers, pointing to the role of Senate opposition in limiting the escalation of the Vietnam war. The press has also at times been of considerable assistance to the movement against the war—for example, Harrison Salisbury's reports on the bombing of North Vietnam, or the printing of the Pentagon papers and the report of the Peers Commission—despite the overall bias of the press towards accepting the assumptions, institutions and practices of American foreign policy.

Instead of trying to reveal the sham nature of existing 'democracy' or 'freedom' by confrontation it is possible to try to demonstrate in practice alternative forms of democracy in workers' control and community control, and to utilize existing freedoms for more radical purposes. Often positive alternatives emerge as part of immediate opposition to a specific evil like redundancy, exploitation of tenants, or racial discrimination. Radical use of existing liberal freedoms has evolved out of the movement against the Vietnam war. The early teach-ins on Vietnam used both freedom of speech and academic values of critical enquiry and debate to clarify the nature of the war, and by implication, the need for opposition. The relevance of the teach-in as a form of political education, and its appropriateness as a response to the continuing escalation of the war, declined. But in the longer-term the Vietnam movement has resulted in the creation of a group committed to radical scholarship on Asia centred around their own journal. The Vietnam movement also promoted its own journalism among opponents of the war engaged in the task of seeking out the truth about peace negotiation offers, the conduct of the war, and the intentions of the administration. The importance of academic experiment and of freedom to publish an independent radical press has been demonstrated in other contexts, for example, the development of experimental art education at Hornsey Art College during the occupation of the college in 1968, and by the enormous range of community, movement, and underground papers (despite the occasional suppression of the latter on the grounds of obscenity). The labour movement has in the past also developed its own journalism—for example, in the 'unstamped press' of the early nineteenth century—and its own scholarship and education, and in doing so widened the scope of press freedom and of education.*

---

* An interesting example of independent use of the mass media is the Pacifica Foundation in the United States, which runs a number of non-commercial radio stations financed by listener-subscription. Pacifica tries to counteract the tendencies of the mass media criticized by Marcuse. It makes available full statements by significant public figures, gives air-time 'to precisely those minority views that the mass media ordinarily screen out', and does so 'generously, regularly, and on the speaker's own terms'. It also gives detailed news coverage. Cultural programmes concentrate mainly on experimental plays, poetry and music.

Thedore Roszak notes in his article on the Pacifica Foundation that: 'In the San

The importance of using and extending existing freedoms rather than rejecting them lies not only in their immediate advantages for a protest movement, but in the significance of liberal values for a future society. If liberal freedoms and the associated values of individualism, rationality and tolerance are simply a historical product of a capitalist society, then they may be discarded under socialism. But if they have a permanent value which transcends their immediate context, then although in a future society their precise meaning and institutional applications may change, liberal freedoms and ideas are not to be devalued in the present. This perspective suggests that the limitations of freedom of speech or of the press arise out of the forms of economic and political control and of the current commercial and political ethos—but these limitations are not proof of the irrelevance of free speech and publication. Their meaning and application in the immediate future might, as already suggested, be partially altered by a coherent radical movement. This approach is half-suggested by Marcuse himself, but he leaves the suggestion in the air as the second part of a 'dialectical proposition': 'And yet . . . the existence and practice of these liberties remain a precondition for the restoration of their original oppositional function, provided that the effort to transcend their (often self-imposed) limitations is intensified' (ibid., 98).

But while Marcuse is half-prepared to accept that political freedoms may be restored to their critical and radical role if used by the Left, he is not prepared to accept the liberal position of indiscriminate tolerance of both the Left and the Right, arguing that ideally the government should discriminate in favour of the Left and against the Right. This would mean denying freedom of speech and publication to militarist, racist or anti-socialist groups, and censorship of teaching in universities. When 'progressive' forces are not in power, the logic of his position leads to the suppression of right-wing speeches and lectures by disruptive action by the Left. Marcuse supports the selective suppression of liberties on the grounds that tolerance is a relative and not an absolute good. Tolerance in contemporary American society has ceased to be progressive, and an ethic of 'tolerance' serves to perpetuate the evils of the system. The philosophical assumption underlying the case for tolerance—that all men are rational, has been undermined by the indoctrination processes of affluent capitalism.*

Francisco Bay area it would be no exaggeration to say that KPFA has become the indispensable element within a vital cultural and political community which the station itself created' (*Anarchy*, no. 93, 327).

* There is a good deal of evidence to support Marcuse's belief that the mass media and the style of American politics operate in such a way as to minimize the possibility of coherent understanding, independent judgment and critical thought—though Marcuse himself does not produce much evidence. For example, in an illuminating

There is a good deal of evidence that the present tendency is to discriminate selectively against the Left—partly because the police tend to
have conservative if not ultra-right attitudes, but principally because the
Left pose a challenge to the whole political and economic organization of
society. Right-wing groups, on the other hand, unless they associate
themselves explicitly with fascism or Nazism, do not pose a visible threat
to the existing establishment. Martin Oppenheimer notes:

> It is interesting that leftists are often blamed for the incursions of
> the right on the democratic process whereas the ultra-right (for
> example, the Minutemen, the Klan) are rarely blamed for 'creating
> an atmosphere of violence' when leftists act illegally (*Urban
> Guerrilla*, 68).

It is therefore arguable that protection of genuine freedom of opinion and
of critical thought means not only the strong defence of civil liberties for
left-groups, but some discrimination in favour of the statement of left-
wing ideas in institutions like the universities. But it does not necessarily
follow that denying a hearing to the Right is either justifiable or prudent.

The immediate dangers of disrupting meetings are suggested by
Michael Harrington in a liberal critique of the tendencies towards 'anti-
libertarianism and elitism' within the movement against the Vietnam
war:

> I am disturbed when the Left proposes to break up public meetings.
> For Lyndon Johnson and Dean Rusk . . . have a right under the
> Constitution of the United States to peaceable assembly. . . .
> I would suggest to the social disrupters that if they take a calm look
> at the relationship of forces in America today, and particularly at the
> control of the forces of repression, they will see that they are creating
> a logic whereby 'those who break up meetings will not be able to
> hold meetings' (in McReynolds, *We Have Been Invaded by the
> Twenty-first Century*, 164).

Lyndon Johnson had of course an automatic access to the mass media so
that his 'right' to make known his views was exceptionally well insured.
Harrington also fails to examine the point that protests directed against
those responsible for governmental policy cannot be seen simply as an

study of the mass media Daniel Boorstin analyses how the news media create
'pseudo events' initiated by or for the media. He comments:

> In a democratic society like ours . . . the people can be flooded by pseudo events.
> For us, freedom of speech and of the press and of broadcasting includes freedom
> to create pseudo events. Competing politicians, competing newsmen, and
> competing news media contest in this creation. . . . Our 'free market place of
> ideas' is a place where people are confronted by competing pseudo events and
> are allowed to judge among them (*The Image*, 45–6).

attack on the right to free speech by individuals. But his fear that these tactics will rebound against the Left is well justified. When the statement of right-wing views is made not by a government spokesman but by a member of the radical Right the question of the freedom of speech arises directly. Despite the fact that far Right views accept many elements in prevailing ideology, and often have supporters in high-ranking political and military circles, to some extent movements like the John Birch Society are in genuine opposition. Moreover, to some extent the far Right is a movement of protest against the establishment, and may share certain values held by the Left—for example, a reaction against the centralization of power, and a nostalgia for earlier democratic and libertarian traditions. And as some of the New Left have recognized, sections of the community supporting right-wing views may themselves suffer from economic exploitation and social deprivation, and have a right to express their dissent.

Marcuse's assumption that the manipulated masses of America and the West are not open to reasoned or moral persuasion, and no form of constructive political change is possible, leads logically to reliance on guerrilla warfare by an alienated élite, aided perhaps by the outcasts of white society. A vanguard committed to wage war against the vast majority of the people is, however, liable to adopt rigid and increasingly unreal attitudes. The Weathermen, for example, came to assume that 80 per cent of the American people were beyond redemption and seriously debated whether little children should be classified as 'pigs'. This kind of approach is not only intolerant, but a-political.

Tolerance and rationalism

Marcuse's insistence that the meaning of tolerance must be interpreted within a specific context, and that it should not automatically be extended to opponents of tolerance, or to inhuman policies, is, however, reasonable. Indeed, his interpretation is implicit within liberal thought. Tolerance is a value rooted in respect for individuality and for the free play of opinion, and an awareness that both personalities and ideas differ. Tolerance may include a positive desire for individual, cultural and intellectual variety, and although as Mill stressed it may be fostered by a degree of indifference, it is not a value-free attitude of total neutrality or indifference. In so far as it is rooted in respect for individuality and cultural variety it cannot logically be extended to policies and actions designed to denigrate or destroy other individuals and cultures. One does not 'tolerate' murder, torture or unjust imprisonment. Neither does one 'tolerate' the humiliation of a whole group—religious or racial. Common-sense awareness of these distinctions leads to the classing of intolerance and explicit religious bigotry or racialism together. (Marcuse obscures his argument by extending his definition of 'tolerance' to mean passive acquiescence in governmental policies.)

Where freedom of speech or other forms of personal freedom conflict with the demands of social tolerance, then governments have been willing to legislate in an attempt to institutionalize the tolerance of discriminated-against minorities, and to ban speech and publication likely to inflame hatred and promote intolerance. Neither is the academic tolerance extended to ideas indiscriminately extended to advocates or representatives of policies which conflict with the other liberal values espoused by universities. Recognition of the value of scientific experiment would not be extended to a doctor who had carried out experiments on concentration camp victims.*

There is also a necessary potential conflict between the espousal of liberal values and the acceptance of majority opinions, since in many societies, cultural attitudes may promote forms of intolerance. It is not therefore necessarily 'élitist' in the sense of intellectual or moral arrogance to oppose majority opinion, as automatic acceptance of the 'will' of the majority would clearly mean abrogating all intellectual and moral standards and independent political judgment. All these points are accepted in the theory of 'liberal democracy'. Where direct action seems illiberal and intolerant is that it moves beyond attempts to persuade the majority verbally to action designed to influence policy directly. Where the policy concerned involves serious discrimination against a section of the population, or the denial of basic freedoms to others, or direct violence against people, then direct resistance may be seen as a means of asserting the principles underlying tolerance. But the attitudes of the resisters to those who oppose them, and the methods they choose, define whether the movement is seeking to promote tolerance in general, or whether it develops its own forms of intolerance. Attempts to limit in general free expression of political ideas—however intolerant the ideas—do promote a specific intolerance.

The deliberate disruption of speeches and lectures by some radical students espousing direct action also reinforces the impression that

---

* This principle is relevant to the incident when students of Essex University prevented a scientist from the Porton Down Germ Warfare Research Establishment from speaking. The Vice-Chancellor sent down three students involved on his own authority without any formal disciplinary hearings. Colin Crouch observes that:

> Few incidents have expressed more dramatically the gulf that exists between the old liberal and the new radical. Where Sloman saw the resolute defence of a value of free society, his student (and staff) opponents saw the arbitrary exercise of undemocratic authority. Where he saw free speech as essential to his university, they saw freedom of speech made a mockery by the fact that governments had the power to control scientists to work in the interests of developing crippling diseases (*The Student Revolt*, 103).

resort to direct action means the abandonment of rational debate. If a movement is described as 'irrational', its irrationalism may lie in its goals, its ideology, its general life-style, or its particular style of action. Liberal critics of student movements often have all these elements in mind, but the only factor relevant here is whether the adoption of 'direct action' is in itself irrational.

Direct action is sometimes assumed to be irrational because the critic is contrasting rationality with emotion. The advocates of direct action do sometimes claim that action which dramatizes a situation, or action which involves voluntary risk and suffering, has more persuasive power than mere words. At a symposium on civil disobedience, Raghavan N. Iyer commented on Gandhi's theory of non-violent direct action:

> Gandhi knew that human beings are not rationally induced to change long-standing prejudices. The appeal to reason is necessary but it is limited. One makes it, but then one must have another form of appeal, and for Gandhi this is the appeal to the heart, to the conscience, decency and moral self-respect of other men. . . . To say that the appeal to reason is inadequate or that the appeal to the heart will involve suffering is not the same as abdicating reason altogether or wholly abandoning concern for human happiness. However, it is true—and I think this is the sovereign difficulty in Gandhi's theory for a number of people who haven't understood his presuppositions or don't share them—that Gandhi could not accept the over-rationalistic assumptions of the eighteenth century (in Freeman, *et al.*, *Civil Disobedience*, 23).

One element in the criticism of direct action does appear to stem from adherence to an 'enlightenment' ideal of liberalism and rationalism, and a Benthamite conception of democracy. Hayden comments that the First Amendment freedoms assume a system in which 'the people can make their needs known to officials and if those needs are not met, replace their officials through elections' (*Trial*, 44). In this context appealing to the emotions looks like discarding rational advocacy and encouragement of irrational forces. Moreover, within the Benthamite model irrationality (which is associated particularly with tradition) is a reactionary force holding up the progress of enlightenment. In later liberal theory irration-alism is seen less in terms of conservative traditionalism than in terms of movements operating outside the parliamentary process, who have abandoned the etiquette of reasoned debate—which is the hallmark of parliamentary politics—for brute force, which threatens to break down the restraints of parliamentary liberalism.

The main reason why direct action is seen to be irrational stems there-fore not from a contrast between rationality and emotion, but from a contrast between rational discourse and direct coercion. Ortega y Gasset defines direct action by associating it with French syndicalism, and then comments that:

> Civilization is nothing else than the attempt to reduce force to being the *ultima ratio*. We are now beginning to realize this with startling clearness, because 'direct action' consists in inverting the order and proclaiming violence as *prima ratio*, or strictly as *unica ratio*. It is the norm which proposes the annulment of all norms, which suppresses all intermediate process between our purpose and its execution. It is the Magna Carta of barbarism (*The Revolt of the Masses*, 57).

William Kornhauser who also associates direct action with mass political behaviour remarks that people 'act directly when they do not engage in discussion on the matter at hand' when they grasp 'those means of action which lie immediately to hand' and 'employ various more or less coercive measures against those individuals and groups who resist them' (*The Politics of Mass Society*, 44–5). This definition combines emphasis on coercion with a picture of mass spontaneity unmediated by reason—a modern version of the mob.

In political argument 'irrationalism' denotes a denial of the speaker's own model of a good and rationally organized polity. Thus the irrational element in direct action is defined by the context in which direct action occurs and the degree to which it is an attack both on the values and the conventions of that institution. For instance, direct action in universities seems more disruptive, more unwarranted and more 'irrational' because it occurs in a context which has been idealized as a place of contemplative calm, removed from political strife, and dedicated to the pursuit of knowledge by rational discourse—where the only passion is that for scholarship. The degree to which a mythical academia is the basis for denunciation of student direct action is nicely illustrated by George Kennan. After quoting Woodrow Wilson on the ideal university, he comments:

> There is a dreadful incongruity between this vision and the state of mind—and behavior—of the radical left on the American campus today. In place of a calm science, 'recluse, ascetic, like a nun,' not knowing or caring that the world passes 'if the truth but come in answer to her prayer,' we have people utterly absorbed in the affairs of this passing world (*Democracy and the Student Left*, 4).

Generally, however, the context is parliamentary democracy. Action which seems to deny the basic values of reason, which flouts the conventions of legitimate political activity, and which often implicitly or avowedly is aimed at overthrowing the parliamentary system becomes in this context irrational. How far rational debate is central to the real workings of a parliamentary system is questionable. But some advocates of direct action have helped to underline the significance of rational argument in parliamentary politics by explicitly associating direct action with a rejection of the rationalism inherent in parliamentary forms. Sorel is the best known spokesman for this point of view. In his advocacy of the syndicalist general strike he emphasizes that the beauty of the general strike is that it is an energizing myth not open to logical refutation.

Sorel also illustrates several other elements in the association of direct action with irrationalism. The liberal associates irrationalism equally with the far Right and far Left, which are assumed to have much in common. Sorel fits neatly into this belief in view of his swing from defending syndicalism to sympathy with the patriotic ultra-right in pre-1914 France. When the New Left erupted on to the political scene in the 1960s its style was so noticeably antagonistic to the bureaucratic organization and the desire for respectability of the major western communist parties, that the most available model was that of fascism. Or else historical comparisons were drawn with student populists or anarchists. Sorel suggests another link between types of anarchism and fascism on the one hand, and of both with the New Left—and that is in his celebration of 'violence'. That the New Left quotes Fanon, and not Sorel, does not allay these fears.

Praise of violence seems to fulfil the worst liberal fears of the dangerous impact of protest movements on the frail structure of reason and tolerance within a parliamentary framework. Indeed, the association of direct action with violence (partly because of the automatic application of a theoretical model which equates all extra-parliamentary action with 'violence') is probably the strongest reason for believing direct action is 'irrational'. In his introduction to Sorel's *Reflections on Violence*, Edward Shils refers to Sorel's 'irrationalist violence' (21, n. 11).

The irrationalism attributed to direct action springs therefore from three oversimplifications. The dichotomy between rationalism and emotion ignores, among other things, the fact that the persuasive power of argument depends not only on its rational content, but also on the authority or passion with which it is delivered. (Conversely the persuasive power of direct action depends on the existence of a good case.) The assumption that direct action means violence has been refuted earlier. The third assumption that all justifiable causes can be adequately pursued through the existing political channels, and therefore that movements bypassing these channels are irrational or illiberal, is explored further in the next chapter.

7 Direct action and democracy

Direct action appears to be a method which inherently favours political participation and direct democracy rather than parliamentary styles of democracy. Paul Goodman suggests in an essay on civil disobedience:

> The vague concept that sovereignty resides in the People is usually meaningless, but precisely at critical moments it begins to have a vague meaning. American political history consists spectacularly of illegal actions that became legal, belatedly confirmed by the lawmakers. Civil rights trespassers, unions defying injunctions, suffragettes and agrarians being violent, abolitionists aiding runaway slaves, and back to the Boston Tea Party—were these people practising 'civil disobedience' or were they 'Insurrectionary'? I think neither. Rather in urgent haste they were exercising their sovereignty, practising direct democracy, disregarding the apparent law and sure of the emerging law (in Goldwin (ed.), *On Civil Disobedience*, 125).

In so far as direct action does embody this conception of popular sovereignty directly exercised, and not mediated by representation, it is antagonistic to parliamentarianism, which is celebrated for the very fact that its democracy is indirect.

Direct action is not necessarily subversive of the existing political system. At a certain level it may be seen as a way of plugging gaps in the system due to inadequate administration, lack of imagination or normal bureaucratic inertia. The squatting campaign fits into this interpretation. Second, direct action can be understood in terms of a pressure group model—as a means of the poor and disadvantaged exercising pressure to protect and forward their own interests because they are denied access to the accepted channels of influence.

But the general tendency of direct action methods is to promote alternatives to the existing parliamentary model and existing modes of administration in the workplace or the university. This aim was quite explicit in the syndicalist theory of reliance on industrial action rather than electoral and parliamentary politics, and in the syndicalist goal of a society run by the trade unions. It has also been prominent in student support for the ideas of workers' control and direct democracy in the universities. Manifestations of a spirit of direct democracy may emerge spontaneously within a mass demonstration or a localized campaign.

Opposition to direct democracy is a modern expression of the nine-teenth-century antithesis between liberalism and democracy: a fear that acceptance of the popular will as 'sovereign' will lead to the curtailment of minority rights or political freedoms, and to the sweeping away of the legal and constitutional bulwarks against the arbitrary exercise of the majority will. Forms of populism threaten the liberal version of democracy which has been grafted on to the constitutional growth of parliamentary institutions, and which has assigned to the electorate at a national level the limited role of choosing between competing élites. Elections then become largely an extension of the system of checks and balances, and a guarantee of peaceful changeover of power.

One of the virtues of this representative system from the liberal standpoint is, as noted in the last chapter, the moderating influence it exerts on politics and its encouragement of compromise. Political parties which are in themselves coalitions of interests are obliged to bid across the board for votes, and to alternate in office with the opposition. Even political parties starting out with more 'extreme' and 'ideological' commitments, like European socialist parties and the British Labour Party, have been educated in the routines of the parliamentary process into accepting gradualism in reform and a moderation of their beliefs. It is precisely because of the compromises inherent in accepting the rules of the parliamentary game that syndicalism evolved at the turn of the century, and that direct action is being espoused now by disenchanted radicals.

Third, there is a fear not only of the ignorance and extremism associated with popular political intervention, but of the dual dangers stemming from 'mob' rule—anarchy and tyranny. The fear of the mob in the eighteenth and nineteenth century took colouring from classical examples of 'mob rule' in the Greek city states, but was based on contemporary examples of mob violence in London or the more frightening revolutionary excesses of the *sans-culottes* in Paris. But an even greater danger to a free and civilized society is seen to stem from the tendency of the mob to submit itself to a single master: the demagogue who becomes a tyrant along the classical Greek pattern, or the plebiscitary dictatorship of the French model.

Finally, in both ancient Greece and modern Europe, rule by the people meant the dominance of the poor and the unpropertied. Concern to preserve a tradition of individual freedom, to maintain civic peace and to preserve the rights of minorities, has undoubtedly also meant a concern to preserve private property and wealth, the order which upholds the existing rule of private enterprise, and the privileges of affluence. These privileges have not been solely economic. The minority also enjoyed the benefits of education, culture and good manners. So that the maintenance of liberalism since the nineteenth century has been associated with upholding certain intellectual and cultural standards and graces of social behaviour against the levelling effects of social equality and 'democracy'.

In this century the 'mob' has been largely replaced by the notion of the 'masses'. This reflects in part a sense that sheer numbers of people have increased, and that the 'masses' must triumph as a result of an inherent physical force. Ortega y Gasset's reflections in the 1920s are informed by a despairing certainty that intellectual and cultural distinction, political moderation and liberal freedoms are under irresistible attack from the masses. The masses have occupied the centre of the stage as the old local and communal ties which bound them to their assigned place in life have been broken. In their movement the masses sweep away the professionals who used to understand the arts of social and political life. The evolution of mass political movements results from the breakdown of social ties and intermediate loyalties which gave significance and discipline to individual life.

The role of mass or 'totalitarian' movements is closely associated in the liberal vision with direct action. Ortega y Gasset makes the link explicit:

> When the reconstruction of the origins of our epoch is undertaken, it will be observed that the first notes of its special harmony were sounded in those groups of French syndicalists and realists of about 1900, inventors of the method and the name of 'direct action' (*The Revolt of the Masses*, 56–7).

When the masses take part in public life it has always been through direct action, which sweeps aside the conventions of parliamentarianism—and of civilized society. 'The political doctrine which has represented the loftiest endeavour towards common life is liberal democracy.' It is founded on respect for others and 'is the prototype of "indirect action" '.

More recent writings link 'direct action' to the rise of mass movements and associate both with fascism. The connection between Sorel's 'philosophy of direct action' and later movements is made by Kornhauser, who claims Sorel 'influenced such mass movements as revolutionary syndicalism in France, as well as many totalitarian movements, such as fascism in Italy, nazism in Germany, and Communism in Russia' (*The Politics of Mass Society*, 46). This statement is historically inaccurate, but reflects how all 'extremist' movements are bracketed together as a threat to liberal parliamentarianism. (A few lines later the Industrial Workers of the World is bracketed with the Ku Klux Klan as a mass movement resorting to violence.) Kornhauser's model is relevant to this discussion not for its depiction of direct action, but for its delineation of an ideal of liberal society and parliamentary democracy.

He notes that direct action occurs when men act outside the communal groups or associations in which they are open to mutual persuasion. If they act within their natural interest groups then they will on an issue like high taxes try to change the law through propaganda, electoral pressures, and financing lobbyists. He also draws on Schumpeter's analysis of how the individual's sense of reality and responsibility decline as issues become more remote from his immediate interests and concerns, and his personal knowledge and observation.

> In the realm of public affairs there are sectors that are more within the reach of the citizen's mind than others. This is true, first, of local affairs. . . . Second, there are many national issues that concern individuals and groups so directly and unmistakably as to evoke volitions that are genuine and definite enough. . . . However, when we move still farther away from the private concerns of the family and the business office into those regions of national and international affairs that lack a direct and unmistakable link with those private concerns, individual volition, command of facts and method of inference soon [decline] (ibid., 44).

Kornhauser concludes that mass behaviour 'involves direct, activist modes of response to remote symbols'. He also argues that political activism 'denies respect for principles of free competition and public discussion as the basis for compromising conflicting interests'. Finally it is undemocratic 'because it abrogates institutional procedures intended to guarantee both majority choice and minority rights'.

The pluralist conception of society and politics, the role of the citizen in relation to national and international policy, and the nature of political compromise are all relevant to the question of whether the indirect modes of parliamentary democracy are better than direct democracy, and if so at what level. They also all have a bearing on possible uses of direct action.

Pluralism and 'mass behaviour'

Pluralism is both an élitist and democratic doctrine, depending on the model envisaged. The first conception stresses the role of an independent aristocracy in curbing central power, and in safeguarding local and communal liberties. It is based on an interpretation of feudalism. Democratic pluralism shares with its predecessor a constitutional belief in communal powers as a curb upon centralizing despotism, but lays greater stress on popular political participation, and on political activism as the exercise of freedom and as the means of safeguarding it. The two models are nicely blended in De Tocqueville's *Ancien Régime*, whilst *Democracy in America* is a conscious attempt to analyse a wholly democratic form of pluralism. This democratic model does not rest on the particular privileges and virtues of an élite, but on the diversity and vitality of different communities and other forms of local association. The underlying model for De Tocqueville is the New England town meeting.

The logic of the democratic pluralist approach suggests support for local direct democracy. It also suggests the relevance of popular control in the factory, the school, or the tenants' association. Belief in the importance of individual political responsibility and of communal action might also be extended to justify locally based direct action on issues like housing, traffic and pollution. Emphasis on local power could also provide justification for local disobedience to central government policies regarded as tyrannical or inappropriate to the needs of the community. Such action also meets Schumpeter's criteria of direct personal knowledge and personal interest as a measure of the realism of political judgments.

However, the pluralist model put forward by Kornhauser is not based principally on the inherent values of political activity or on the values of community, but on the need for stability, and for political moderation. He is wary of the radicalism engendered by strong community ties among mining or fishing communities. His pluralism is primarily a pressure group model, and participation in local associations is a means of anchoring the individual to the institutions and cultural values of the political system. Local political involvement is designed to subserve 'pluralism' at the intermediate level—the level of competing businesses, professional associations, trade unions, and other interest groups. Local activity is also necessary to maintain electoral and party politics and to provide legitimacy for the institutions of liberal democracy. If an active minority is not prepared to raise funds, canvass votes or stand for local or national office, and if a substantial proportion of the population is not prepared to vote, then mass apathy threatens the system as a whole.

Kornhauser's model of intermediate pluralism also ensures that democracy remains largely indirect. Pressure groups themselves are comparatively centralized, and the individual who participates by collecting signatures to a petition or by financing a lobbyist in Washington is not exerting a direct influence on the administration or on Congress. The multiplicity of competing pressure groups is also assumed to ensure that the government and Congress will in turn be protected from excessive influence by one particular grouping. Kornhauser's theory requires both that the citizenry be insulated against the seductive calls to extremism by demagogues, and that the ruling élites be protected from direct pressure from below. He accepts Shils's assessment of McCarthyism as a mass movement which 'sought to attack policy and personnel of the Army, State Department, *New York Times*, and Harvard University' (ibid., 103).

The category of 'mass behaviour' which is used to contrast with the American pressure group model is an unreal construct, partly because it tries to link 'activism' with a lack of community ties, and with irrational attachment to 'remote symbols'. It is totally inappropriate to an understanding of the direct action movements which arose after Kornhauser's book was written in the 1950s. Direct action to remedy immediate and personal problems or injustices—including the high taxes opposed by the Poujadists whom Kornhauser cites—does not usually spring either from a lack of community ties or from a lack of personal involvement. Superficially, movements against the H-bomb seem closer to examples of 'mass behaviour' since the issue involved is remote and also emotive. But the two relatively serious studies so far made of the British CND both refute this hypothesis. Frank Parkin set out to test Kornhauser's model, and came to the conclusion in his book *Middle Class Radicalism* that the average adult member of the CND tended to be active in local politics and voluntary bodies, well informed on political matters, and unusual mainly in a tendency to hold mildly unorthodox views on a spectrum of issues.

Christopher Driver observes in a discussion of proposals for alternative forms of defence that:

> It is entirely characteristic of this country that one of the most suggestive and wide-ranging studies to have been initiated in this field is . . . a symposium which arose out of a couple of local peace conferences in Colchester early in 1961. . . . Such a phenomenon itself partially contradicts any attempt to interpret CND and its offshoots in the terms used by Kornhauser in his *The Politics of Mass Society.* . . . The Campaign as a whole, in its local aspects, is if anything a testimony to the surviving strength, in Britain, of subsidiary political 'publics' and groupings (*The Disarmers*, 239).

An adequate understanding of movements like CND would require examination not only of who took part but why the issues involved were conducive to 'extremist' views. The category of 'extremism' is as questionable as that of 'mass behaviour', and the ideal of political compromise requires further analysis.

The role of compromise

In British and American political discourse 'compromise' has acquired almost entirely positive connotations. It suggests adapting to the realities of the political situation, meeting opponents half-way, and promoting the public good by sacrificing some personal demands or preferences. It is also associated with the liberal values of reason and tolerance. As Raymond Aron has pointed out, in other languages the word for compromise has more offensive overtones—in German, for example, the equivalent is *kuhhandeln*, which is like the American 'horse trading' (*Democracy and Totalitarianism*, 48).

American political vocabulary includes a number of terms indicating political deals involving the crude pursuit of interest. But the link between 'horse trading' among interest groups and the more exalted idea of compromise, which suggests a sublimation of interests through the mediation of reason, has not harmed the reputation of compromise. The adjudication of competing interests after the American pattern has been widely accepted as a necessary element in a liberal democratic system and a guarantee of both freedom and democratic rights. Daniel Bell notes that: 'The saving grace, so to speak, of American politics, was that all sorts of groups were tolerated, and the system of the "deal" became the pragmatic counterpart of the philosophical principle of toleration' (*The End of Ideology*, 112).

Compromise in the abstract is largely meaningless. In some senses compromise is necessary to all forms of political activity, just as co-operation is necessary; since all politics requires people to work together, and no form of politics can be explained solely in terms of domination. But the precise implications of compromise depend on the institutional context and the issues involved.

Compromise between competing interests is only advantageous if the interests are legitimate. Moreover, a fair bargain between two competing groups may still be made at the expense of a wider community. The idea of an equilibrium of pressure groups creating a situation of maximum satisfaction is as unreal as the idea of the automatic regulation by market forces, and rests on the same unrealistic assumption that perfect competition prevails between equal units. It also makes the same mistake of assuming that competition can ensure an overall social good when in practice there are no pure 'interest' groups which are committed to the good of the whole. Groups promoting public 'causes' are excluded from the pressure group theory based on an analogy with the market, and in practice (with certain exceptions) are excluded from political influence.

Compromise in the Anglo-American model is also often associated with the (effectively) two-party system, in which the parties are themselves coalitions of interests, and in which policies are put together by a process of adjustment. The stability and moderation resulting is seen as another virtue of compromise politics—since one of the implications of compromise is that it avoids 'extremism'. The idea of compromise is therefore closely associated with the idealization of liberal democracy as a middle-ground between fascism and communism, which by eschewing their ideological commitments and their methods preserves freedom and parliamentary institutions.

The built-in flaw in this model is that political processes which promote compromise and gradual reforms necessarily favour those who have most power and privilege in society. The impatience with parliamentary socialist parties arises from the conviction that parties which become parliamentary over time cease to be socialist, and that even a party in power is, so long as it accepts the rules of the game, hampered at every turn by the business and financial institutions, and by the conduct of its own civil service, or the attitudes of the armed forces. Similarly, any group suffering from discrimination which accepts the ethos of gradualism and compromise is accepting a gradualism in escaping from discrimination.

Direct action can be seen as a partial method of altering the conservatism inherent in the parliamentary approach, because it can challenge the economic and social forces which influence the political process. The evolution of trade unions, and of the strike as the central method of industrial action, represents one attempt to create some form of counter-power in an arena of conflict outside parliamentary politics. Direct action may also be seen as a means of pressurizing a government into exerting its legislative and executive capacities in order to promote the interests of a particular group. Third, direct action can be used as a form of mass resistance to particular governmental policies—as British trade unions briefly demonstrated in 1972 when dockers were sent to jail by the Industrial Relations Court for illegal picketing. At times the potential of resistance can be used not against the government, but in support of it in response to a military or economic threat—like the general strike used in Germany in 1919 to defeat the attempted Kapp Putsch.

Direct action can therefore be incorporated into an acceptance of parliamentarianism, if it is seen as a means of setting limits to compromise, and of altering the context in which decisions are taken. It may do both by altering the configurations of power, and by changing certain beliefs, attitudes and interpretations of the situation. In contrast with the resort to guerrilla warfare, a direct action campaign is usually open at all stages to a negotiated settlement which involves a degree of compromise; though where a head-on confrontation like the general strike occurs, one side has to accept defeat.

Apart from its potential for effecting social change direct action is also a means of asserting the importance of certain values in politics. Idealization of compromise in general obscures the fact that whilst adjudication of two legitimate sets of interests may be necessary and desirable, there can also be an undesirable compromise of basic values or principles. How far political activity can or should be guided by moral principle is itself a complicated and controversial question—especially in the realm of inter-state relations, since politics is the art of the possible bounded by necessity. But the concept of politics requires belief in an area of free and conscious choice. It also embodies belief in certain values intrinsic to an ideal of free political activity. Whilst commitment to parliamentary democracy means, if the implied values are taken seriously, a rejection of domination and pure violence and of extreme forms of fraudulence, trickery and corruption. Direct action which is intended to assert an uncompromising stand on principle is an attempt to give substance to moral considerations liable to be lost in the day-to-day 'realities' of government, or to be obscured by propaganda.

Whether or not the assertion of moral considerations is politically desirable depends, like the virtues of compromise, on the context. It also depends on what sort of moral principles are being asserted. Where ethical or religious commitments are a source of inter-communal conflict, or a guise for the domination of one section of the population over the rest, practical considerations of interest may conduce more to the public good than excess spiritual zeal. Even if the principles being asserted are political —for example, equality of right—there may be a genuine conflict between the remedying of injustice and the stability of the state. Lincoln is often praised, for example, because before the American Civil War he insisted that maintaining the Union was even more important than abolishing slavery. But where moral issues are being totally subordinated to *realpolitik*, or where the appeal to 'freedom' and 'democracy' is held to justify totally ruthless military and political operations, then protest centred on the morality of both ends and means is important in redressing the balance.

Direct democracy

So far direct action has been considered as a supplement or corrective to parliamentary politics. But in democratic terms it can be justified because it introduces an element of 'direct democracy', by enabling individuals to make a direct impact on the decision-making process at a regional, national or even international level. It may also—especially in community-based campaigns—promote organizational forms of direct democracy at a local level.

The characteristic of direct democracy is that it gives direct power to the majority, without elaborate restraints on that power; and that decisions are taken in assembly, subject to the immediate pressures of public opinion and feeling. Where the group is bound together by common interests and problems—as were early American settlers in the West,* or as residents in a particular neighbourhood are today, then the possibility of direct democracy being viable is high. A shared political and moral culture clearly also assists a sense of communal interest. But the danger of injustice exists because in a conflict of interests or ideas the majority can

* For an account of the early American experience of direct democracy see Daniel Boorstin, *The Americans*, on the self-government of companies trekking west, the 'Claim Clubs' formed by settlers and the miners' camps, which were 'remarkable for the spontaneity, localism, and independence with which they developed their laws'. Boorstin comments:

> For most of the early age of Western settlement—from the first decades of the nineteenth century at least until the Civil War—'Club Law' was the law of the transient West. It had its faults, but they were not the faults of bureaucracy, technicality, or legalism. Club Law, like Vigilante Law, meant popular justice, quick remedies, lay procedures, and rule of thumb (vol. 2, 104–5).

carry the day solely on the basis of personal gain and not in terms of a 'general will'; or because in the passion and uncertainty of the moment, people are swayed to take a rash decision. The case for constitutional limits on the extent of popular sovereignty rests on the reasonable conviction that the temporary will of a majority does not necessarily coincide either with an objective standard of justice recognized by that society, or with the real long-term interests of the majority. In a simple and localized direct democracy this drawback is mitigated by its very flexibility; if the people repent at leisure the means are at hand for a rapid reversal of the decision.

The danger of direct democracy at the level of a popular assembly is extended by analogy to the national sphere, though what is involved here is not popular decision, but popular pressure on the decisions made by the legislature or government. The advantages or drawbacks of such 'populist' pressures can best be assessed by examining the main reasons given for favouring indirect democracy.

The most potent in the past has been the fear of the masses, allied to belief in the need to uphold minority standards of intellectual judgment and to lead the way in enlightened reforms despite majority prejudice. Roy Hattersley, M.P., argued, for instance, in an article that modern populism:

> finds a ready audience among the distressed, the discontented, and the dispossessed. They are pathetically willing to blame their conditions on the traditional populist demons. Immigration has become their most celebrated cause. Westminster politicians, insulated from the realities of ordinary political life, have, they believe, no idea what the public really feels about immigration (*Guardian*, 28 December 1971, 10).

But populist movements have not always been illiberal. David McReynolds notes that at the end of the last century American populism had its strongest base in the South:

> And, while the Populist movement eventually foundered on the rock of racism, the true story is that the dirt-poor farmers, the 'crackers' and 'rednecks' of Georgia and elsewhere, made a conscious effort to build an alliance with the Negroes, and, together, attempted to break the political power of the so-called aristocracy. . . . If the Populist movement failed, as it did, it is nevertheless true that, at its high point, it forged a genuine link between poor white and poor Negro, and it is also true that the same Northern forces that today categorize the South in such bitter terms for lacking any real sense of liberalism were, then, terrified of the Populists and rejoiced in their downfall (*We Have Been Invaded by the Twenty-first Century*, 63).

Since the intellectual rejection of 'populism' in the 1950s by scholars who saw it as backward-looking, a 'paranoid' style of politics, and as a 'nativist' and anti-Semitic movement, a number of historical studies have begun to restore to American populism its respectability in scholarly eyes, and its radicalism.* American populism has also reasserted itself as a political force which manifested itself most strikingly in the Democratic primaries. Its present political ambivalence is illustrated by the support given to Wallace as well as to McGovern—both rebels against the Party establishment and the existing conventions of politics. But the majority of the new populists supported McGovern.

There is also a case to be made that the most serious examples of illiberalism manifested in political policies are not primarily the product of populist agitation, but are sanctioned and fostered by the government, and promoted from within the legislature and administration. Powellism flourished in a period when successive governments were restricting immigration and creating a 'respectable' context for openly racist utterances. McCarthyism was nurtured by the respectability of anti-communism, the existence of ready-made institutions like the HUAC, and the initial lack of significant political opposition.

McCarthyism can be understood in terms either of a manifestation of the excesses of 'democracy' or as the result of too little democracy. In a recent analytical study of civil liberties in the United States William Spinrad summarizes the two views. To Edward Shils, leading exponent of the élitist view of McCarthyism, it represented:

> an intervention of the 'mass society', especially its most alienated
> representatives, into the private provinces of elites. The result was a
> politicizing of issues that should best be left to gentlemanly discourse,
> that is, of bringing into the public arena what should be kept within
> the elite 'clubs'. The antidote was the assumption and an
> assertion by the elites of their right to function without external
> annoyance. . . . The 1954 censure of Joseph McCarthy by the
> 'elite' senators, including many traditional 'conservatives', was hailed
> as both a verification of this analysis and a specimen of the type of
> counter tactics advocated (*Civil Liberties*, 170).

Spinrad considers that this analysis reflected a particular kind of theoretical commitment and exaggerated the importance of McCarthy himself and his supporters—so that McCarthyite tactics were treated as aberrations in the system, not as aspects of it. 'In fact the very existence of the cold war as the essential and necessary condition for all that happened was mentioned by several analysts only in passing' (ibid., 169). Spinrad also argues, against Shils's preference for secrecy, that one of the

* See, for example, Cunningham (ed.), *The Populists in Historical Perspective*.

most pervasive and oppressive aspects of McCarthyism was the secrecy and uncertainty which surrounded security probes and blacklisting.

Whether or not the people's representatives and those within the administration are more liberally inclined than the majority of the electorate will depend in part on the nature of the political system and the prevailing political climate. At present it can be guaranteed that some of the most illiberal attitudes and beliefs will be given expression, and weight, through representative and governmental organs in the United States and in Britain. It can also be argued that if there is a threat of fascism, it is from within the ranks of the government—especially the security and armed services. Army dossiers on Congressmen are indicative of this kind of threat, as Democratic Representative Abner J. Mikva commented in an interview with a reporter from the *Progressive* in February 1971. The reporter asked what purpose a dossier on him might serve. Mikva replied:

> I've puzzled about that. So far as I can see, there are only two reasons, and both of them sound so *Seven Days in May*-ish that I don't like to think about them.
>
> One purpose would be served if there were ever some kind of a military *putsch* in this country. The people who had been kept under surveillance would be the ones singled out for arrest and removal from the scene.
>
> The second purpose occurred to me when the former agents described some of the activities they had been directed to keep track of, such as my public speeches. . . . Perhaps they wanted to compile evidence to be used in some future military court— evidence that I was disloyal to the military establishment because I suggested that we cut manpower by ten per cent last year (19).

The reporter commented that Mikva referred to these conjectures 'as *Seven Days in May*-ish' but seemed to take them seriously. Mikva responded:

> Well, I do now. . . . The problem . . . is that the military can completely lose sight of the overriding principle of a democracy: that the civilians are to run the military for the sake of the country, rather than have the military run themselves—and the country— for their own sake (ibid.).

Another reason for indirect democracy is that many decisions facing government are so specialized that they require detailed technical knowledge, and are too complex to be decided by a simple majority vote in the manner of a referendum. From the point of view of efficient government, therefore, ultimate decision on issues like entry into the Common Market should be left to the government. Where complicated negotiations are required popular decision seems even less appropriate. In the areas of defence and foreign policy the plea that the complexity of the issues precludes intelligent assessment by those outside the charmed circle is particularly popular. Indeed, requirements of secrecy and security often mean that even the elected representatives are excluded from the necessary knowledge and the opportunity of debate.

But some popular debate and decision on matters of broad policy and principle are particularly needed in these spheres. People's lives may be more fatally affected by defence decisions or foreign commitments than by many internal policies. The government may also commit greater crimes. Popular dictation of the *detailed* implementation of policy is clearly impossible as well as undesirable, whether through the populist device of the referendum or through mass direct action. Popular opinion can call on the government to stop nuclear tests or withdraw from Vietnam, it cannot indicate how to negotiate and monitor a test ban treaty, or how to phase troop withdrawal.

The well-known and accepted idea of a division of responsibility and of spheres of decision between a legislature and an executive can be extended to create a third sphere appropriate to popular decision on national issues. This notion already exists rather hazily in the idea of a popular 'mandate', but is obscured by the multiple functions of elections. It is also embedded in the existence of the freedom to dissent and in the conception of the press acting as a 'fourth estate'. Direct action on national and international issues is a tentative attempt to give some substance to the democratic right to influence government policy. It falls between formal gestures of dissent which can be safely ignored (as a petition can be filed away) and the last resort of actual rebellion (though it may occasionally approach that stage). It is rather a right to resistance and to the positive assertion of certain demands—a popular sanction equivalent to the legislature's right to withhold funds or vote down legislation. (The ability to vote a government out of office is a more generalized check on corruption and mismanagement, and a very rough and ready endorsement of promised future policies—it is not an adequate sanction in relation to particular policies.)

This model could be defended as an approach towards increasing the reality of popular sovereignty, even in a political system which could claim to be genuinely representative of popular opinion. However, as Kennan asserts, the more political institutions serve as 'a vehicle for the will of the majority', the less necessary it is for the unsatisfied to resort to the 'primitive' form of self-expression involved in 'calling attention to themselves and their emotions by mass demonstrations and mass defiance of established authority' (*Democracy and the Student Left*, 15). And, indeed, populist movements have in the past tried to fashion devices—like primaries and referenda initiated from below—to promote the expression of the popular will, and to obviate manipulation and corruption of both the electoral process and of the workings of the legislature.

There is no doubt that in varying degrees, as Kennan concludes, mass demonstrations in the United States indicate a fairly widespread sense that the existing system is no longer adequately representative or responsive to popular opinion. The discovery by those who voted for Johnson in 1964, in the expectation that he would avoid escalation of the Vietnam war, that during the campaign he had already planned to bomb North Vietnam underlined disillusionment with the whole political process.* The triumph in 1968 of the Democratic Party machine, personified by Mayor Daley, over the grass roots support for Eugene McCarthy, was another blow to those trying to work through the Party. But the unexpected degree of support gained by McGovern in the 1972 primaries indicated both how widely dissatisfaction with the old political style had spread, and the potential for adapting the existing party organization to represent new popular attitudes.

Irresponsible government

Perhaps even more important than the responsiveness of government to popular opinion is the question of whether it is capable of implementing policies which have popular support, or of maintaining its claim to responsible direction of public affairs. In America, the disintegration of the cities, the crisis in the ghettos and the problems of pollution all underline the failure of federal, state and local government. In Britain the threat of combined inflation and unemployment, the housing shortage and profiteering by developers, and the problems of transport and traffic also illustrate the relative impotence of government.

Aside from more complex causes, three main reasons can be given for weak government. First, but least significant, is the fact of corruption, which applies particularly in the governing of many American cities. Second is the nature of bureaucratic administration, which not only baffles the ordinary citizen but tends to render ineffective those involved in its own workings. A nice example was given during the publicity early in 1972

---

* See, for example, the bitter comments by McReynolds:

> I and many others on the democratic Left voted for Johnson. Our support was critical and limited, but it was real. We broke our backs to get as heavy a vote as possible for Johnson because Goldwater was the front man for the radical right. . . . We fought our good and rational political fight and defeated Goldwater's war policy. . . . We defeated the reactionary domestic policy of the GOP and have seen the poverty fight cut to shreds. There are now 500,000 dead Vietnamese and 15,000 dead Americans—most of them killed since we won our striking victory at the polls. A victory 'that clearly proved' that democratic political processes can defeat reaction. Let us pray God we never endure another such victory (*We Have Been Invaded by the Twenty-first Century*, 168–9).

about the dumping of cyanide and other lethal chemicals by industry. The *Sunday Times* on 16 January 1972 revealed that: 'This appalling state of affairs was outlined *two years ago* by an expert report of a technical committee. . . . The report called for a watchdog authority to ensure that industry deals responsibly with its solid waste materials' (3). Hannah Arendt explains the anger and frustration of radical protests as a response to the 'transformation of government into administration, or of republics into bureaucracies', and the resulting sense of impotence when 'there is nobody left with whom one can argue, to whom one can present grievances, on whom the pressures of power can be exerted' (*On Violence*, 81). But the particular nature of bureaucratic rule in the West can only be understood in relation to the third, and most important, reason for government incapacity in many circumstances. That is, as Justice Douglas stresses in his brief essay on *Points of Rebellion*, the supreme influence of big business corporations and of the business ethos.

The role of business interests can be seen at a local, national and international level. A minor but telling illustration is provided by the redevelopment of Covent Garden in the centre of London, a scheme which the Covent Garden Community Association was founded to fight. The *Guardian* reported on 27 June 1972:

> Developers have started work on 25 acres of Covent Garden . . .
> the GLC says officially that plans for the area are still in the
> melting pot and that there is 'now a pause while everyone waits to
> see'. The reality is that the developers are not waiting. . . . In
> collaboration with the GLC planning team, developers are
> clearing sites and building in anticipation of the Comprehensive
> Development Area plan being largely approved (17).

A London planner told a *Guardian* correspondent on 1 August 1972, 'Planning control is not very extensive at all. The commercial development field, with its finance, can call the tune' (14).

At the international level there is a growing literature on the role played by giant corporations. Ghita Ionescu reviewing two books on this subject asks whether the nation-state can 'still contain the corporations'. He notes that 'only recently, we have seen Ford choosing across the nation-states over which its multi-national estate extends the territorial site for new projects and grading States according to their industrial, economic, and political propitiousness' (*Guardian*, 11 March 1971, 7). Kornhauser's picture of an intermediate level of pressure group activity, including business interests, is therefore well removed from the reality in which corporate interests tend to be dominant (with the willing compliance of most of those involved in government). The evolution of the European Common Market, despite popular fears of losing power to the bureaucrats of the EEC Commission, is primarily an acceptance of this trend towards increasing the scope and competence of the big corporations.

The present intermeshing of business and administration in the USA is suggested by the role of advisory committees. An article in the *Progressive* notes:

> In today's Washington the most expansive and least visible branch of government is the advisory committee. There are two or three thousand of them; no one has more than fragmentary data on their number, membership, meetings and activities. The most influential are composed exclusively of top officials of large corporations. They meet regularly with Administration leaders, . . . assign company personnel to prepare governmental reports, listen to the decision-makers and help them decide things.
>
> Press and public interest groups are often barred from the committees' formal meetings (November 1971, 28).

The National Petroleum Council, for example, set up under Truman, has been cited by Professor Robert Engler as 'a case study of how an advisory committee takes advantage of its quasi-governmental privilege to concentrate its economic power and use it for political purposes' (ibid., 29).

The largely unrestrained power of big corporations makes it impossible for the actions of the government to be considered solely in terms of an ideal of representative government. But since in many cases direct action is resorted to by a minority, and the government can claim at least tacit support from a majority of voters for its own policy, there is a genuine question in terms of democratic theory whether a minority should use extra-constitutional tactics to oppose local or national authority. Kennan observes that: 'willingness to accept, in principle, the workings of a system based on the will of the majority, even when you yourself are in the minority, is simply the essence of democracy' (*Democracy and the Student Left*, 15).

Minority rights and the majority will

Whether a minority is justified in taking direct action against the wishes of the majority depends on the question of equality of right, and on how far the vital interests of a minority may be held to outweigh the more general-ized interests or preferences of a majority. The principle of equality of right applies to issues of basic voting rights or civil rights—even if a majority wishes to withhold them—because the principle of democracy implies a universalization of the right to vote and to political equality. Moreover, a minority suffering from active discrimination can appeal to the safeguarding of minority rights enshrined in the 'liberal' theory of democracy. A minority committed to particular religious beliefs is usually held to have a right to observe practices which may be disliked by the majority, provided they do not violate fundamental social principles or the laws of the land. Similarly, gypsies might claim that their right to pursue their livelihood and way of life in peace, even if they offend the local residents.

The most topical and most important issue on which minority rights are said to conflict with majority interests is that of industrial action. It is particularly obvious that in this field the issue is not simply one of a minority versus the majority; since industry is not controlled by the government but, for the most part, by independent employers, conflicts which occur are usually between the interests of the employers and those of their workers. In addition some sections of the business world—as the role of developers in Britain illustrates—clearly exploit 'the community' much more directly than any trade union. Furthermore, the rhetoric of British politicians and mass media which tends to picture a minority of unionists holding 'the public' up to ransom, obscures the fact that a substantial proportion of the working population are in trade unions. Press treatment also tends to portray the business world—especially industrialists responsible for exports—as representatives of a pure public interest.

Despite all these considerations it is true that the Conservative government elected in 1970 had pledged itself to 'reform' industrial relations, and so it could claim some kind of very generalized 'mandate' for its Industrial Relations Act. And whilst some strikes which cause direct hardship to society as a whole, like the miners' strike of 1971, appear to have support from other unionists and non-unionists, other strikes which directly inconvenience the public may not. In the first instance the trade unions could reasonably claim that the Industrial Relations Act deprived them of a number of basic trade union rights precariously won in the past, which are necessary for their freedom of organization and their ability to protect their basic interests. In the second instance, trade unions can fairly argue that every other section of society, including the professions, are engaged in a similar competitive struggle which is dictated by the nature of the economic and social system; that the fact that unions are singled out for blame is a reflection of the ideological slant of the system; and that union abstention from pressing wage claims would not in itself better the lot of the poorest paid workers or of old age pensioners, and would not even necessarily curb inflation. Nevertheless, it is true that unions still tend to accept the ethos of the old craft unionism—maintaining the standards and the differentials of their members without concerning themselves unduly about the less privileged work force (for example, many women workers) or the non-unionized unemployed. Neither have they been willing to challenge the economic system itself, or the discrimination practised by society against its coloured citizens or immigrants. Since the Second World War American unions have in the hands of their leadership become one of the most reliable supporters of the establishment.

It is therefore possible that a more radical and egalitarian stance by the trade union movement, a greater willingness to think in terms of direct democracy in industry and of the relationship between the unions and the underprivileged sections of society, would also be more constructive and more fully justifiable in terms of social equality and the genuine 'public interest'.

Democracy has been defined in this discussion to include concern for minority rights because it is inherent in the idea of rule 'by the people for the people' that all have equal claims, and that rule should be designed for the welfare of all. Majority decision is the fairest rule-of-thumb procedure to hand, but majority domination is contrary to the aim of equal participation by citizens in governing, and to the equality of rights. By natural extension—and this usage of the term democracy was common in the nineteenth century—equality of political rights suggests a wider economic and social equality. So although this interpretation of 'democracy' embodies the liberal emphasis on the rights of minorities, it does not imply (as liberalism has often done) that the freedom of minorities should be used to protect minority privileges which are damaging to the majority. In any particular situation the rhetoric of 'rights' may obscure the reality of privileges being defended; and certain forms of direct action—particularly non-co-operation with government policies designed to promote educational or social equality—could fall into this category.

Slightly different considerations prevail if a minority is pitting itself against majority opinion on an issue of foreign policy or defence. They could (as noted in chapter 5) justify their actions in terms of overriding universal moral principles, or in terms of international law. But they could also argue in some cases that the principles of democracy have an application which extends beyond national frontiers. In any colonial situation, once the colonial people are seen to have human rights, colonial rule is not justified because it has majority support within the colonizing power, if the majority of those under colonial rule want independence. Thus in debates about the Vietnam war the beliefs and wishes of the Vietnamese were accepted by both sides as being of central importance in terms of the justification of the war. The degree of democracy which could—or could not—be claimed for the Saigon regime was also accepted as relevant.

Once the question of democracy in other countries is considered there is a very substantial amount of evidence to suggest that governments who stress democratic precepts at home tend to subordinate them to economic or military interests in their international policies. Because it is now the major western imperial power, in recent years the United States has most obviously pursued a policy based on military and economic aid to pro-

American dictatorships, and on CIA subversion of regimes threatening American business or military interests. One of the most interesting parts of the International Telephone and Telegraph Corporation scandal, unearthed by Jack Anderson early in 1972, was not the bribing of the Nixon administration, but the revelation of ITT letters to the CIA suggesting forms of economic pressure to bring down President Allende's popularly elected Marxist government, and canvassing the possibility of an uprising by selected members of the armed forces. A minority of Americans came to the conclusion in the late 1960s that the American brand of imperialism made a mockery of its claim to respect democratic principles—and that their dissent was a form of representation of the people whose lives might be shaped, and destroyed, by American power; and whose voices clearly were not heard by the men in the inner governmental councils.

Furthermore, once the commitment to democratic principle is lost in one sphere it tends to be lost in others, and the methods employed overseas may be brought home. The corroding effects of the Indo-China war and then the Algerian war on French politics are well known; French troops became specialists in torture; parliamentary democracy was discredited and was replaced by Gaullism; and a *coup d'état* by the 'ultras' in the French army was narrowly averted. America's Indo-China war has similar dangers; the enormous scope and power of the armed forces and security services was briefly indicated in the last chapter, and their power is maintained and enhanced by the defence and foreign policies pursued by successive Presidents.

In the realm of foreign and defence policy there are also grounds for doubting that the elected representatives—whether the President or Congress, have full knowledge or control of the decisions being made. Even the Vice-President, for example, is not informed about the activities of the CIA. The Pentagon made clear to the Senate in June 1972 that its price for accepting the Strategic Arms Limitation agreement to limit the numbers of offensive missiles, and of missile defences, was the investment of billions of dollars in new technological development in offensive weapons.

Where direct action is a response to the usurpation of power from the elected representatives it may be seen primarily as an attempt to re-create a form of representative democracy, rather than as an attempt to alter the workings of the representative system, or to replace it altogether. But even an attempt at restoration, of what is any case a partially mythical past, is in the present necessarily radical. Moreover, awareness of domination by military or business forces tends to encourage commitment to decentralized community, direct democratic control, and to anti-militarist and anti-capitalist goals. The logic of using direct action does therefore lead to seeking the demise of parliamentary democracy within a free enterprise economy, and of parliamentary liberalism as it has so far been known and understood; though by no means all those who embark on direct action will follow this logic to its conclusion.

Conclusion

The previous three chapters argue that direct action can be justified by constitutional, liberal and democratic principles if the existing institutions cease to embody these principles. If the radical implications of constitutionalism, liberalism and democracy are extended direct action can be seen as an intrinsically valuable mode of expressing independence, practising resistance and exercising popular sovereignty.

However, direct action itself is a method of opposition, even when it takes constructive forms like the work-in or the reverse-strike, or when it serves as a focus for community feeling. Organizational forms of direct democracy may spring from a direct action campaign, but they have to be maintained and elaborated beyond a period of protest. Direct action may also have a radicalizing effect on those who take part in it (though this depends on the nature of the movement as well as the action), and it may stimulate new ideas. But it does not in itself provide any form of political theory.

Direct action is primarily a way of expressing rebellion. It creates a potential for social change by releasing new energy and determination and encouraging social imagination. But the direction it takes depends on the nature of the movement it is associated with—on the values, the ideas and the organization which promote action and which result from it. This direction can be destructive, or lead to self-indulgence and irrelevance. Or direct action may be institutionalized, as the trade union movement has institutionalized the strike, and so lose its characteristics of rebellion. Or the impact of direct action may achieve results—but the results be limited reforms. Even if direct action does develop into full rebellion, the ideas and organization may be lacking to ensure lasting and fundamental change.

The role played by direct action is therefore necessarily limited to opposition. But this role is one of central importance wherever oppression or injustice exists. In many regimes resistance is the only means of asserting freedom or practising democracy. The parliamentary and pressure group methods available in the 'liberal democracies' of the West have not rendered direct action unnecessary. Though these constitutional channels increase the range of activity open to the individual citizen or underprivileged communities, effective protest and opposition often requires the use of direct action. And without effective opposition changes toward a better society are impossible.

The present range of dissent—from individuals sailing into a nuclear testing area to prisoners sitting-in to assert their right to human dignity—and the prevalence of direct action methods in dissent, contain both risk and promise: the risk and promise of greater democracy.

Bibliography

AMERICAN FRIENDS SERVICE COMMITTEE (1971), *Indochina 1971*

ARDAGH, JOHN (1970), *The New France*, Penguin

ARENDT, HANNAH (1970), *On Violence*, Allen Lane: The Penguin Press

ARON, RAYMOND (1968), *Democracy and Totalitarianism*, Weidenfeld & Nicolson

BEDAU, H. A. (ed.) (1969), *Civil Disobedience*, Pegasus, New York

BELL, DANIEL (1965), *The End of Ideology*, The Free Press, New York

BELL, INGE POWELL (1968), *CORE and the Strategy of Nonviolence*, Random House, New York

BENEWICK, ROBERT (1969), *Political Violence and Public Order*, Allen Lane: The Penguin Press

BOORSTIN, DANIEL (1963), *The Image*, Penguin

BOORSTIN, DANIEL (1969), *The Americans*, vol. 2, Penguin

BUCKMAN, PETER (1970), *The Limits of Protest*, Gollancz

BURNS, W. HAYWOOD (1964), *The Voices of Negro Protest in America*, Oxford University Press

CANTOR, NORMAN (1970), *The Age of Protest*, Allen & Unwin

CARMICHAEL, STOKELY and HAMILTON, CHARLES V. (1968), *Black Power*, Jonathan Cape

CHOMSKY, NOAM (1972), *Problems of Knowledge and Freedom*, Fontana

COCKBURN, ALEXANDER and BLACKBURN, ROBIN (eds.) (1969), *Student Power*, Penguin

COHN-BENDIT, DANIEL and GABRIEL (1969), *Obsolete Communism: The Left-Wing Alternative*, Penguin

COLE, G. D. H. (1925–7), *A Short History of the British Working Class Movement*, vols I–III, Allen & Unwin

COLE, G. D. H. and POSTGATE, RAYMOND (1963), *The Common People 1746–1946*, Methuen University Paperbacks

CONANT, RALPH W. (1971), *The Prospects for Revolution*, Harper's Magazine Press, New York

COOK, FRED. J. (1964), *The FBI Nobody Knows*, Jonathan Cape

COOPER, DAVID (ed.) (1968), *The Dialectics of Liberation*, Penguin

CRICK, BERNARD (1964), *In Defence of Politics*, Penguin

CROUCH, COLIN (1970), *The Student Revolt*, Bodley Head

CUNNINGHAM, R. J. (ed.) (1968), *The Populists in Historical Perspective*, D. C. Heath, Boston

DAVIS, ANGELA Y. (1971), *If They Come in the Morning . . .*, Orbach & Chambers

DELLINGER, DAVE (1971), *Revolutionary Nonviolence*, Anchor Books, Doubleday, New York

DOUGLAS, WILLIAM O. (1970), *Points of Rebellion*, Random House, New York

DRIVER, CHRISTOPHER (1964), *The Disarmers*, Hodder & Stoughton

ENDLEMAN, SHALOM (ed.) (1969), *Violence in the Streets*, Gerald Duckworth

FANON, FRANTZ (1965), *The Wretched of the Earth*, MacGibbon & Kee

FAWCETT, MILLICENT GARRETT (1912), *Women's Suffrage*, T. C. and E. C. Jack

FORTAS, ABE (1968), *Concerning Dissent and Civil Disobedience*, Signet Books, New American Library, New York

FREEMAN, HARROP A., *et al.* (1966), *Civil Disobedience*, Center for the Study of Democratic Institutions, Santa Barbara

FULFORD, ROGER (1957), *Votes for Women*, Faber & Faber

GOLDWIN, ROBERT A. (ed.) (1969), *On Civil Disobedience*, Rand McNally, Chicago

GOODMAN, PAUL (ed.) (1964), *Seeds of Liberation*, George Braziller, New York

GUÉRIN, DANIEL (1970), *Anarchism*, Monthly Review Press, New York and London

HAIN, PETER (1971), *Don't Play with Apartheid*, Allen & Unwin

HALLORAN, JAMES D., *et al.* (1970), *Demonstrations and Communication: A Case Study*, Penguin

HAMMOND, J. L. and BARBARA (1920), *The Village Labourer 1760–1832*, Longmans, Green & Co

HAMPSTEAD GROUP, COMMITTEE OF 100 (undated), *Mail Interception and Telephone Tapping in Britain*

HAYDEN, TOM (1971), *Trial*, Jonathan Cape

HENTOFF, NAT. (ed.) (1967), *The Essays of A. J. Muste*, Bobbs-Merrill, Indianapolis

HERSH, SEYMOUR (1972), *Cover-up*, Random House, New York

HUNNIUS, F. C. (1968), *Student Revolts*, War Resisters' International

JACOBS, PAUL and LANDAU, SAUL (1967), *The New Radicals*, Penguin

KENNAN, GEORGE (1968), *Democracy and the Student Left*, Hutchinson

KING, MARTIN LUTHER, Jr. (1959), *Stride Toward Freedom*, Gollancz

KING, MARTIN LUTHER, Jr. (1964), *Why We Can't Wait*, Signet Books, The New American Library, New York

KORNHAUSER, WILLIAM (1960), *The Politics of Mass Society*, Routledge & Kegan Paul

LYND, STAUGHTON (ed.) (1966), *Nonviolence in America: A Documentary History*, Bobbs-Merrill, Indianapolis

MACHIAVELLI, NICCOLO (1950), *The Prince and the Discourses*, The Modern Library, Random House, New York

MCREYNOLDS, DAVID (1970), *We Have Been Invaded by the Twenty-first Century*, Grove Press, New York

MILIBAND, RALPH (1961), *Parliamentary Socialism*, Allen & Unwin

MITCHELL, DAVID (1967), *The Fighting Pankhursts*, Jonathan Cape

MORGAN, CHARLES, Jr. (1964), *A Time To Speak*, Harper & Row, New York

NATIONAL COUNCIL FOR CIVIL LIBERTIES (1968), *Handbook of Citizens' Rights*

NEVILLE, RICHARD (1970), *Play Power*, Random House, New York

NEWMAN, EDWIN S. (1970), *Civil Liberty and Civil Rights*, Oceana Publications, New York

OPPENHEIMER, MARTIN (1970), *Urban Guerrilla*, Penguin

ORTEGA Y GASSET, JOSÉ (1961), *The Revolt of the Masses*, Unwin Books, Allen & Unwin

PANKHURST, CHRISTABEL (1959), *Unshackled*, Hutchinson

PANKHURST, E. SYLVIA (1931), *The Suffragette Movement*, Longmans, Green & Co.

PARKIN, FRANK (1968), *Middle Class Radicalism*, Manchester University Press
PRIESTLY, HAROLD (1968), *Voice of Protest*, Leslie Frewin
RAMELSON, MARIAN (1967), *The Petticoat Rebellion*, Lawrence & Wishart
ROCKER, RUDOLPH (undated), *Anarcho-Syndicalism*, Modern Publishers, Indore, India
RUBENSTEIN, RICHARD (1970), *Rebels in Eden*, Little, Brown & Company, Boston
RUDÉ, GEORGE (1962), *Wilkes and Liberty*, Oxford University Press
SEALE, BOBBY (1970), *Seize the Time*, Arrow Books, Hutchinson
SEGAL, RONALD (1970), *America's Receding Future*, Penguin
SKOLNICK, JEROME H. (ed.) (1969), *The Politics of Protest*, Simon & Schuster, New York
SOREL, GEORGES (1961), *Reflections on Violence*, Collier Books, New York
SPINRAD, WILLIAM (1970), *Civil Liberties*, Quadrangle Books, Chicago
STONE, I. F. (1968), *In a Time of Torment*, Jonathan Cape
SYMONS, JULIAN (1959), *The General Strike*, Cresset Press
TAYLOR, TELFORD (1970), *Nuremberg and Vietnam*, Quadrangle Books, Chicago
THOMPSON, ANTHONY A. (1970), *Big Brother in Britain Today*, Michael Joseph
THOMPSON, DOROTHY (ed.) (1971), *The Early Chartists*, Macmillan
THOMPSON, E. P. (1965), *The Making of the English Working Class*, Gollancz
THOMSON, DAVID (1961), *England in the Nineteenth Century (1815–1914)*, Penguin
URQUHART, CLARA (ed.) (1963), *A Matter of Life*, Jonathan Cape
WASKOW, ARTHUR I. (1967), *From Race Riot to Sit-In, 1919 and the 1960s*, Anchor Books, Doubleday, New York
WILLIAMS, RAYMOND (1965), *The Long Revolution*, Penguin
WOLFF, ROBERT PAUL, *et al.* (1969), *A Critique of Pure Tolerance*, Jonathan Cape
ZINN, HOWARD (1965), *SNCC: The New Abolitionists*, Beacon Press, Boston

Index

Date Due